D1713295

Historical Dramas of Alfred de Musset

To Harry & Jolie,
With love and best wishes,

Dad / Dave

Currents in Comparative Romance Languages and Literatures

Tamara Alvarez-Detrell and Michael G. Paulson
General Editors

Vol. 46

PETER LANG
New York • Washington, D.C./Baltimore
Bern • Frankfurt am Main • Berlin • Vienna • Paris

Historical Dramas of Alfred de Musset

Translated by
David Sices

PETER LANG
New York • Washington, D.C./Baltimore
Bern • Frankfurt am Main • Berlin • Vienna • Paris

Library of Congress Cataloging-in-Publication Data

Musset, Alfred de, 1810–1857.
[André del Sarto. English]
Historical dramas of Alfred de Musset/ translated by David Sices.
p. cm. —(Currents in comparative Romance languages and literatures; vol. 46)
Includes bibliographical references.
Contents: Andrea del Sarto—Lorenzaccio.
1. Sarto, Andrea del, 1486–1530—Drama. 2. Medici, Lorenzino de', 1514–1548—Drama. 3. Florence (Italy)—History—1421–1737—Drama. I. Sices, David. II. Musset, Alfred de, 1810–1857. Lorenzaccio. English. III. Title.
PQ2369.A73E5 842'.7—dc20 96-130
ISBN 0-8204-3143-5
ISSN 0893-5963

Die Deutsche Bibliothek-CIP-Einheitsaufnahme

Musset, Alfred de:
[Historical dramas]
Historical dramas of Alfred de Musset/
transl. by David Sices. –New York; Washington, D.C./Baltimore; Bern; Frankfurt am Main; Berlin; Vienna; Paris: Lang.
(Currents in comparative Romance languages and literatures; Vol. 46)
ISBN 0-8204-3143-5
NE: Sices, David [Übers.]; Musset, Alfred de: [Sammlung <engl.>]; GT

The paper in this book meets the guidelines for permanence and durability of the Committee on Production Guidelines for Book Longevity of the Council of Library Resources.

Printed in the United States of America.

Table of Contents

Introduction

Filippo Would you deny the history of the entire world?...
Lorenzo I don't deny history. I just wasn't there.
Lorenzaccio, V, 2

Alfred de Musset's literary work abounds in contradictions: his abiding reputation as one of the major French Romanticists, vs. his attack on the romantic æsthetic in the name of classical tradition, constitutes only the most pervasive of them. But another significant contradiction can be found in his historical tragedies. It is true that he managed to complete only two of them, quite early in his career; but one of those—*Lorenzaccio*—is probably the most successful and enduring of the entire genre, certainly the most frequently produced on the French and international stage.[1] Its ultimate message, however, is, paradoxically, the meaninglessness of history.

The major practitioners in France of Romantic historical drama—Ludovic Vitet, Alexandre Dumas *père*, Victor Hugo—had essentially a dual purpose: to bring the Romantic historical vision inspired notably by the example of Sir Walter Scott onto the stage as well as into the novel, and to create a serious new theater, capable of displacing from the stage of the Comédie-Française the traditional French "classical" tragedy, whose neo-Aristotelean rules, perfected by Corneille and Racine, had been brought forward into those times by numerous epigones. The Romantics' aim was a tribute to the importance of the official French theater in their day. The 1830 début of Hugo's *Hernani* in that temple of classicism, celebrated in Théophile Gautier's *Les Jeunes-France* and Albert Besnard's famous painting, and recounted ever afterward in French manuals of literary history, marked the triumph and perhaps the high-water mark in France of the Romantic movement. But Musset had a different end in view, particularly following the fiasco of his *La Nuit vénitienne* in performance at the Odéon later that same year. So when he wrote his two completed historical tragedies, *Andrea del Sarto* and *Lorenzaccio*, in 1832 and 1833, he did not have stage performance in mind: their inclusion in a volume entitled *Un Spectacle dans un fauteuil*, "An Armchair Show," makes it clear that, at least for the moment, Musset was thinking in terms of an ideal stage, more flexible, more intimate, and in the final analysis more spectacular than anything then conceivable at the Comédie-Française or in the French theater in general. His imagination, both poetic and dramatic, was thus freed from the limitations of contemporary stage practice and resources. On the other hand, however, unlike a Shakespeare, a Racine or a Molière, he was not granted the possibility of seeing his plays take shape in their natural medium, of modifying them on the basis of their audiences' response, of developing his own dramatic instinct in the give-and-take of the theater. When the time came to produce *Andrea del Sarto* in 1848, those revolutionary days were not right for politically "irrelevant" drama, and Musset himself, who had lost the freshness of vision that led him to create his greatest plays in his early twenties, was tempted into modifications to suit the requirements of the "real" stage. As for *Lorenzaccio*, it was not to be mounted until 1896, almost forty years after the author's death, and even then in a severely altered version commissioned by Sarah Bernhardt as an addition to her list of travesty roles: the reduction from five to four acts, with a far smaller cast and the elimination of most subplots, denatured Musset's original dramaturgy.

Musset's conception of historical drama is situated somewhere between those of Ludovic Vitet's *Scènes historiques*,[2] which attempted to dramatize real historical events and thereby render them accessible to a broader public, and historical tragedies like Victor Hugo's *Hernani* and *Ruy Blas*, which used historical characters and events as a background for essentially fictional heroes. *Andrea del Sarto*, which, according to Musset's brother, Paul, was derived from "the abridged notices accompanying the engravings in the *Musée Filhol*,"[3] takes the celebrated Italian renaissance painter as its artist-hero or anti-hero. *Lorenzaccio*, drawn from Benedetto Varchi's 16th-century chronicles, *Storia fiorentina*, via a historical sketch by George Sand, uses historical personages as its primary characters, although it interprets those characters, as well as the events they were involved in, according to Musset's own notion of history.

It is perhaps not surprising that two dramas written at such proximity in Musset's creative development, both drawn from events in the life of renaissance Florence, should share a common historical perspective, even though they are very different in scope and realization. *Andrea del Sarto* is about half *Lorenzaccio*'s length and has proportionally even fewer characters; more importantly, it lacks the complexity of plot, characterization, and theme to be found in the latter play. Dealing with the artist as failure because of love, a common theme throughout Musset's work (its best example is perhaps to be found in the short story, "Le Fils du Titien"[4]), *Andrea del Sarto* tells the story of the artist's final days. Like Robert Browning's well-known poem dating from over a decade later, Musset's play takes its view of the painter, directly or indirectly, from the one propagated by Giorgio Vasari in his *Lives*: most notably that the artist squandered his talent and misused funds given him by the King of France because of excessive infatuation with his wife, Lucrezia del Bene, and a lack of will-power. Musset treats Lucrezia more sympathetically than does Browning, and invents a disciple and friend of the artist, Cordiani, who betrays him with Lucrezia and, at the end of the play, flees with her from Florence as news comes of Andrea's suicide (also invented by the Romantic Musset, in place of the artist's later premature death from the plague). Balancing this more sympathetic treatment of Lucrezia and her lover, Musset views Andrea as the survivor of a glorious generation—that of Leonardo, Michelangelo[5] and Raphael—whose heroic example is giving way to the mannerists' petty imitations. In fact, modern scholarship has tended to see Andrea del Sarto as a master of the rising mannerist generation, rather than the morally and artistically decadent heir of earlier artists, and to emphasize the appreciation that he and his work benefitted from in contemporary Florence, not to mention Italy, France, and the rest of Europe, rather than the inglorious penury and oblivion alleged by Musset, in conformity with Vasari.

From the point of view of the twenty-two-year-old Musset, Andrea del Sarto's fortyish age at death must have seemed rather advanced, making Lucrezia's betrayal of him with a younger man understandable, if not forgivable. In any case, love and betrayal more often than not go together in the author's works. The conflict between love and artistic creation is another that informs a great number of those works, as well. Anticipation of failure became Musset's most characteristic literary theme; in fact, it extended even to the circumstances of his life. We cannot help remembering Flaubert's epistolary comment to Louise Colet, twenty years later: "Musset will have been a charming youth, and then an old man."

Lorenzaccio, as I have said, is a far more complex work. Like *Andrea del Sarto*, it takes an historical figure as its protagonist; also like the earlier work, it treats history with considerable liberty in pursuit of its themes. But it is far less single-minded: apart from the increased number of characters—about thirty-five—and scenes—thirty-eight—in its five acts, involving a large number of different sets, it is marked by greater psychological complexity in its principal characters; its action, centering around the historically factual assassination of Duke Alexander de' Medici by his cousin, Lorenzo de' Medici, in 1536,[6] is in reality a multiple, interwoven set of three main plots and several subordinate ones.[7] The story of Lorenzaccio's[8] conspiracy to murder his cousin, in order to restore a republican form of government, is mingled with two related plots (in both senses of the term): one by Filippo Strozzi and his family to avenge an insult made to his daughter, Luisa, and incidentally to restore the oligarchic form of republic that had formerly existed in Florence; and one by Ricciarda Cibo to win Duke Alexander over by her love to a more enlightened, less despotic and brutal form of rule. Through these various plots, which culminate, in the fourth act, in Lorenzo's murder of the Duke, followed by the inactivity on the part of the "republicans" that he had foreseen, are entwined the successful machinations of Cardinal Cibo, Ricciarda's brother-in-law, to maintain control over the city; the impotence of Florentine noblemen and churchmen in the face of Alexander's despotism and death, and of his succession by Pope Paul III's instrument, Cosimo de' Medici; the vain imprecations of Florentine exiles as they set out for life elsewhere; commentaries on all these events by two Florentine burghers, as well as by two poet-tutors who are willing to celebrate whatever form of government seems to be in power; the futile efforts of young students to reclaim their traditional political rights (this has been seen as a reflection of recent events in France, during the Revolution of 1830); and the fright of an idealistic young painter at the bloodthirsty language he hears Alexander and his bodyguard use as he is painting the Duke's portrait.[9] The artist-as-hero was in vogue at that time—Balzac had published his *Chef d'œuvre inconnu* in 1831—but Musset's artists, in both *Andrea del Sarto* and *Lorenzaccio*, already express a broadly autumnal, disillusioned view. That Musset was deliberately "dedramatizing" his story, and emphasizing thereby the lack of political or moral significance of Lorenzo's act, is made clear at the end of the play, where he chooses to conclude his action with a disappointing, prosaic address, submissive to the real powers, translated almost verbatim from Varchi's chronicle, and spoken "in the distance" toward the populace massed offstage.

Musset's great historical drama, *Lorenzaccio*, can still speak eloquently to the modern reader or playgoer, beyond its important dramatic innovations, through its very contemporary themes: both the denial of historical meaningfulness that permeates it, expressed succinctly in the epigraph at the head of this introduction, and its political and psychological analysis of a city occupied by foreign forces, represented in the play by the German soldiers who hold the Citadel and control Florence in the name of the Emperor and the Pope. The latter may provide an explanation for both increased French interest in the play at the end of the second World War and its choice for a major production by the Za Branou Theater of Prague following the invasion of Czechoslovakia by Soviet tanks in 1968. Although the play offers little hope of meaningful political action in the face of despotism, it is one artist's moving representation of and response to tyranny, and its "unheroic" hero possesses thereby a certain tragic grandeur in the face of power and men's willingness to bow to it.

Lorenzaccio thus goes well beyond Musset's elegiac vision of the artist in society in *Andrea del Sarto*. The two historical dramas taken together, however, represent a considerable artistic achievement, particularly on the part of so young an author, and deserve to be better known outside the linguistic borders of their nation. In my translations of these two plays, I have attempted to remain faithful to the language and style of the original French texts, while making them read—or play—as far as possible as if they had been written in English. I have included only those notes essential for an understanding of the works and their historical sources. Anyone concerned about plumbing more deeply the relationship of Musset's dramatic text to what is currently known of historical truth is referred either to relevant historical manuals or to the works indicated in the selected bibliography at the end of this volume.

Alfred de Musset's two major historical dramas—or tragedies—date from well before his brief, sporadic affair with the great classical actress, Rachel.[10] His efforts to create modern neo-classical tragedies for her to star in at the Comédie-Française, around 1851, were never brought to fruition—of *Faustine* only a few scenes were written out fully, and of *Le Comte d'Essex* there is only a brief scenario—and so are not included here.

I wish to thank the Office of the Dean of the Faculty of Dartmouth College for a financial grant to help with publication of this volume. Above all, as in the case of my translation of Alfred de Musset's *Comedies and*

Proverbs, I particularly want to express my deep appreciation for the invaluable and constant assistance given to me in my work by my wife, Jacqueline Boulon Sices.

Andrea del Sarto

Written in late 1832 and early 1833—although Musset's brother, Paul, later claimed that detailed plans for the drama went back to 1830[1]—*Andrea del Sarto* was first published, like most of the author's dramatic works, in François Buloz's *Revue des deux mondes* (1 April 1833); it was thus the first of all his major writings to be published there. The play was reprinted, essentially unchanged, in the second "*livraison*" of *Un Spectacle dans un fauteuil*[2] ("An Armchair Show"), toward the end of 1834. Although less than a year separates it from the writing of *Lorenzaccio* and Musset's major comedies, it was by common agreement, in Léon Lafoscade's words, "without doubt the nearest to Romantic drama": that is, to the dramatic principles of Victor Hugo's *Cénacle*—with which the young author had only recently parted company—despite its being written in prose.

Andrea del Sarto was the first of Musset's mature plays to reach the stage. On 21 November 1848, the Comédie-Française mounted a production whose run was immediately cut short by political events: the Revolution of 1848. When revolutionary fervor had cooled down, the play received another production, with some help from Musset's connections in high places: this time at the Odéon, premiering on 21 October 1850. It is not said to have gained more than a *succès d'estime*. The psychological and æsthetic interest of Musset's artist-hero was no longer very relevant. In addition, critics blamed the author for liberties he had taken with history: in accordance with Musset's views at the time of the play's writing and with his enduring temperament and ideas, Andrea was transformed into a figure who represents the artist as hero and as lover, betrayed by personal weakness of will and by those around him. The historical figure portrayed by Giorgio Vasari (and, in his wake, Antoine-Michel Filhol, whose *Galerie du Musée Napoléon*[3] was claimed by Paul, the author's brother, as Musset's stimulus to writing the play[4]), was a supremely gifted but weak-willed man whose excessive love for his unworthy wife, Lucrezia di Baccio del Fede, led him to dereliction of professional and moral ethics and to abandoning the lucrative patronage of King Francis I's court in France; furthermore, he squandered on his wife funds entrusted to him by the king for the acquisition of art works upon his return to Florence, thereby forfeiting any chance of recovering Francis's good graces. Vasari and Filhol relate Andrea's death by plague at the age of forty-five, abandoned by a faithless wife. Musset instead turns this death into a suicide in the contemporary Romantic vein, to permit the action to take place over a brief space of time,[5] and he invents a key figure in his drama, Andrea's pupil, Cordiani, whose requited passion for an idealized Lucrezia leads to the couple's betrayal and abandonment of the master. Filhol's moralizing condemnation of the weak-willed painter, as in Vasari's *Lives*, is thus turned into a far more sympathetic, albeit pathetic portrait of the artist in Musset's play.

As was to be the case with all his plays staged during his lifetime, as well as others for which he nourished hopes of production, Musset modified his original text of *Andrea del Sarto*[6] for presentation, further regularizing the work in accordance with theatrical practice of the time (e.g., dividing it in two acts instead of three and setting all the action in the same garden). Since the author's changes were intended primarily to adapt his dramatic vision to the linguistic and moral conventions and the limited scenic capabilities of the contemporary stage, as with several of his *Comedies and Proverbs*, I have used the text published in *Un Spectacle dans un fauteuil* as the basis for my translation.[7]

Cast of Characters:

Andrea del Sarto	a painter
Cordiani	a painter, Andrea's pupil
Damian	a painter, Andrea's pupil
Lionel	a painter, Andrea's pupil
Cesario	a painter, Andrea's pupil
Gremio	Andrea's gatekeeper
Montjoie	a French nobleman
Mathurin	Andrea's servant
John	Andrea's servant
Paolo	the del Fedes' gatekeeper
A doctor	
Lucrezia del Fede	Andrea's wife
Spinetta	Lucrezia's maid

Painters, servants, etc.

Florence
ACT ONE
Scene 1.

Andrea's house.

(A courtyard with a garden at the rear.)

Gremio *(emerging from the gatekeeper's house)* I really thought I heard someone walking in the courtyard. That's a funny thing at four in the morning. Hmm! hmm! What could that mean? *(He comes forward; a man wrapped in a cloak jumps down from a ground floor window.)* That's Miz[8] Lucrezia's window! Stop, whoever you are!

Man Let me go or I'll kill you! *(He stabs him and flees into the garden.)*

Gremio *(alone.)* Help! Murder! Stop, thief! John, help me!

Damian *(coming out in his bathrobe.)* What is it? What have you got to shout about, Gremio?

Gremio There's a thief in the garden.

Damian You old fool! You must be drunk.

Gremio I saw him jump down from Miz Lucrezia's window, right from her window. Look, I'm wounded! He stabbed me in the arm with his dagger.

Damian You are joking! Your cloak is scarcely torn. What is this story you are making up, Gremio? Who the devil could you have seen jumping from Lucrezia's window at such an hour? You ass, you had better not go and tell that to her husband.

Gremio I saw him just like[9] I'm seeing you now.

Damian You have been drinking, Gremio. You are seeing double.

Gremio Double! I only saw one of them.

Damian Why are you waking up the entire house before dawn? A house like this one, too, full of young men and servants! Did someone pay you to make up this crazy story about my best friend's wife? Here you are shouting "Stop thief," and you claim someone jumped out of the window? Are you mad or has someone paid you? Speak up, answer me, let me hear you out.

Gremio My Lord! Jesus Christ! I saw him, it's the God's own truth, I saw him. What have I done to you? I saw him.

Damian Listen, Gremio. Take this purse—it may be lighter than the one that you were given to make up that story. Go drink my health. You know I am your master's friend, don't you? I am certainly no thief; I have no part in any robbery that might be committed against him, do I? You have known me for the ten years I have known Andrea. Well, Gremio, not a word about this. Drink my health. Not a word, do you hear, or I shall have you dismissed. Come on, Gremio, go back to your room, my old friend. Forget the whole thing!

Gremio I saw him, I swear on my own head and on my father's. I saw him with my own eyes. *(He goes back in.)*

Damian *(alone, goes toward the garden and calls out)* Cordiani! Cordiani! *(Cordiani appears.)* Are you mad? Have you come to this? Your friend and mine, poor old Andrea!

Cordiani She loves me, Damian; she loves me! What can you say to me? I am a happy man. Look at me, she loves me. I have been running around this garden since yesterday, I have thrown myself into the damp weeds, I have been striking the statues and the trees and covering the grass she trod with wild kisses.

Damian What about the man who found you! What can you be thinking of? What about Andrea? Andrea, Cordiani!

Cordiani What can I do? Perhaps I am guilty, perhaps you are right. We shall talk more about it tomorrow, some day, later. Let me be happy. Perhaps I am wrong, perhaps she doesn't love me. It is a passing fancy, yes, just a passing fancy and nothing more. But let me be happy.

Damian Nothing more? And you can break a twenty-five year bond like a straw? You can come out of that bedroom? "Perhaps you are guilty?" And the bed-curtains that closed about you are still trembling around her? And the man who sees you come out cries "Murder"?

Cordiani Oh, my friend, how beautiful that woman is!

Damian Madman! Madman!

Cordiani If you only knew what a world I am living in! How the mere sound of her voice makes new life boil up in me! How tears well up in her eyes when she sees something fine, tender, and pure like herself! Oh, my God! Happiness is a sublime altar. May my soul's joy rise up to you like sweet incense. Damian, the poets are mistaken. Was the spirit of evil a fallen angel? It was the spirit of love that, after the creation, refused to leave the earth and, while his brothers were flying back up to heaven, let his golden wings crumble into dust at the feet of the beauty He had created.

Damian I shall talk with you at some other time. The sun is rising; in an hour someone else will come and sit on this bench; like you he will place his hands over his face and it won't be tears of joy that he will be hiding. What are you thinking about?

Cordiani I am thinking of the dark corner in a certain tavern where I have sat so many times, ruing the way I have spent my day. I am thinking about Florence awakening, the walkways, the passers-by who meet, the world which I have been wandering around for twenty years like an unburied ghost, those empty streets I walked through in the depth of the nights, driven by some sinister purpose; I am thinking of my work, my days of discouragement; I spread my arms and see the phantoms of the women I have possessed going by, my pleasures, my sorrows, my hopes! Oh, my friend, how all that has been shattered!

How everything that was seething in me has been blended into a single thought: loving her! It is as if a thousand fragments scattered in the dust had come together in a ray of sunlight!

Damian What can I tell you? What use are words once the action is done? A love like yours knows no friends.

Cordiani What did I have in my heart until now? Thank God, I never sought after knowledge. I wanted no honors, I never gave a center to the immense circles of my thought; I never let anything into it but love of the arts, which is the incense on its altar but not its god. I have earned my living with my paintbrush, with my labor; but my labor nourished only my body; my soul still felt its divine hunger. I placed the whip with which Christ scourged the moneylenders from the temple on the threshold of my heart. Thank God, I never fell in love, my heart has clung to nothing until it was hers.

Damian How can I express all I feel in my heart? I see that you are happy. Are you not as dear to me as he is?

Cordiani And now that she is mine, now that I can let the mad verses telling her of my love flow like sweet tears, and I almost feel an enchanting specter leaning over my shoulder behind me to read them; now that I have a name on my lips—oh, my friend, what man on earth has not seen a cherished being, created for him, meant to live for him, appear a hundred, a thousand times in his dreams? Well, then, what if just one day on earth you should meet that being, hold her in your arms, and then die!

Damian All I can say to you, Cordiani, is that your happiness terrifies me. The important thing is for Andrea not to know!

Cordiani What does that mean? Do you think I seduced her? That she thought about it and I thought about it? For a year I have seen her every day; I talk to her and she answers me; I make a gesture and she understands. She sits at the keyboard, she sings, and I, with my lips parted, watch a tear fall in silence on her bare arm. By what right should she not belong to me?

Damian By what right?

Cordiani Be still! I am in love and I am loved. I do not want to analyze anything or know anything. The only happy people are children who pick a fruit and bring it to their lips, without thinking of anything but that they want it and it is within their grasp.

Damian Oh, if you were here in my place and you were judging yourself! What will the man say to the child, tomorrow?

Cordiani No! No! Am I coming from an orgy, so the morning air strikes my face? Is love's rapture a carousal that vanishes with the night? You standing there, Damian, how long have you seen how I love her? What have you to say now, you who remained silent, you who for a year saw every throb of my heart, every minute of my life going out from my body to join with her? So I am guilty today? Why am I so happy, then? And what can you say to me that I have not said to myself a hundred times already? Am I a heartless rake? Am I an atheist? Have I ever spoken disdainfully of all those sacred words that have vainly passed over men's lips since time began? I have reproached myself in every possible way and still I am happy. Remorse, awful revenge, mute and dismal sorrow, all those fearsome specters have come to stand on my doorstep. Not one of them was able to overcome my love for Lucrezia. Be still! The doors are opening. Come into my studio with me. There, in a room closed to all eyes, I have carved in purest marble the image of my beloved. I will only answer you in its presence. Come along with me. The courtyard is filling up with people and the academy is going to open. *(Exeunt.—Painters cross the courtyard in all directions. Lionel and Cesario come forward.)*

Lionel Is the master up yet?

Cesario *(singing.)*

To work the whole day long,
Paint pictures like the dickens,
Ding dong, ding dong,
Our good old Master Strong,
To work the whole day long,
He rose up with the chickens.

Lionel There once were so many pupils in this academy! How we would argue over one man or the other! The creation of a new picture was such an event! Under Michelangelo the schools were actually battlefields. Now they are scarcely filled, slowly, with silent young men. People work to make a living and the arts are becoming trades.

Cesario That is the way everything under the sun passes. I found Michelangelo boring. I am just as glad he is dead.[10]

Lionel What a genius he was!

Cesario Why, yes, he was a genius. Now he should let us be. Have you seen Pontormo's[11] picture?

Lionel Yes, for me it is a sign of the times: a man undecided amid a thousand different paths, caricaturing the great masters, drowning in his own enthusiasm. He would be capable of hanging on to Albrecht Dürer's[12] gothic mantle to save himself.

Cesario Long live the gothic! If the arts are dying, antiquity won't bring anything back to life. Tra la la! We need something new.

Andrea *(entering, speaking to a manservant:)* Tell Gremio to saddle two horses, one for him and one for me. We are going out to the farm.

Cesario *(continuing)* New things at any cost, anything new! Well, master, what is new this morning?

Andrea Always in a good humor, aren't you, Cesario? Everything is new this morning, my child. The trees, the sun and the flowers, and it will all be new again tomorrow. Only men get older, everything gets younger around them every day. Good morning, Lionel. Up so early, my old friend?

Cesario So the young painters are right, then, to ask for something new, since nature herself seeks it for herself and grants it to all.

Lionel Do you realize who you are speaking to?

Andrea Ha! ha! Arguing already? My good friends, argument is a sterile soil, believe me. That is what kills everything. Fewer prefaces, more books. You are painters, my children. Let your mouths be silent and your right hand speak for you. Listen to me, though, Cesario. Nature indeed always seeks to be new; but she always stays the same. Are you one of those who would like her to change the color of her dress, and the woods to turn blue or red? That is not the way she sees things. Beside a withered flower grows another flower just like it, and thousands of families can be recognized under the dew in the sun's first rays. Every morning, the angel of life and death brings a new jewel to the mother of us all, but all her jewels are alike. The arts should strive to be like her, since they are nought save through imitation! Every century may see new customs, new fashions, new ways of thinking; but genius should be as unchanging as beauty! Young hands, full of strength and vitality, should grasp the sacred torch from the shaking hands of old men! They should guard that divine flame from the breath of the winds, so it will pass through future centuries as it has done through those gone by! Will you remember that, Cesario? And now go and paint. To work! To work! Life is so short! *(He pushes him into the studio.—To Lionel:)* We are growing old, my poor friend. Youth no longer wants us. I do not know if it is because our world is a new-born infant or an old man fallen into second childhood.

Lionel God's blood! Your newcomers had better not give me too much back-talk! I shall end up wearing my sword while I work.

Andrea That is just like you, my good Lionel, with your dagger-thrusts! The only ones they kill today are those who are already dying. The time for swords is past in Italy. Come along, my friend, let the chatterers talk and we shall try to keep abreast of our time until they come to bury us. *(Enter Damian.)* Well, my good Damian, is Cordiani coming today?

Damian I don't think he will be coming, he is ill.

Andrea What, him ill! I saw him last night and he wasn't. Seriously ill? Let us go see him, Damian. What can be the matter with him?

Damian Don't go see him, he could not receive you. He has shut himself in for the entire day.

Andrea Oh, no, not for me. Come along, Damian!

Damian Seriously, he wants to remain alone.

Andrea Alone, and ill! You frighten me. Has anything happened to him? A quarrel? A duel? He is such a violent man! Oh, my Lord, whatever can it be? He hasn't let me know. He has been wounded, hasn't he? *(To the painters who have remained and are waiting for him:)* Excuse me, my friends... but, as you know, he is my childhood friend, he is my best and my most faithful comrade.

Damian Rest assured, nothing has happened to him. A slight fever; you will see he is all better tomorrow.

Andrea I hope to God! Oh, how often I have prayed to heaven for so dear a life to be preserved! Let me tell you, my friends: in these times of decadence that Michelangelo's death[13] has left us in, I have placed my hopes in him. He has a hot head but a warm heart. Providence does not let such abilities go astray!

How many times, behind his back, I have felt my breast swell as he climbed up and down his ladder with his palette in his hand, and I have stretched out my arms, ready to clasp him to my heart, to kiss his brow, so young and so candid, from which genius radiated in every direction! What ease! What enthusiasm! But what an austere and heartfelt love of truth! How often have I thought with delight that he is younger than I! I looked sadly on my own poor labors and said to future centuries, in my heart: this is all I have managed to accomplish, but I bequeath my friend to you!

Lionel Master, there is a man here asking for you.

Andrea What is it? What does he want?

Servant The horses have been saddled. Gremio is ready, my lord.

Andrea All right, I shall bid you farewell. I shall be back at the studio in two hours. But he is not ill? *(To Damian.)* Not seriously, is he? We shall see him tomorrow? Come on, join us for supper. And if you see Lucrezia, tell her that I am going to the farm and I shall be back. *(Exit.)*

Scene 2.

A grove.

(Andrea at a distance.)

Gremio *(seated on the grass.)* Hmm! And yet I did see him. What reason could he have for saying I didn't? Still, he must have one, since he gave me... *(counting in his palm)* four, five six... The devil take it, there's something behind all this. No, it definitely can't have been a burglar. I did have another idea, but... hold on, that's where I have to stop. "Shut up, Gremio," said I to myself, "hey, no more of this, my friend!" That would be a funny thing to think! Thinking is nothing, what can people see of it? You can think whatever you want. *(He sings.)*

The shepherd saw a stream race by
Down toward the mill, and asked it why;
"Have you seen the lovely miller's lass
Using the pond for her looking-glass?"

Andrea *(coming back.)* Gremio, go put the bridles back on those poor animals. We have to start back on our way; the sun is getting lower now, so we won't be so hot along the way home. *(Exit*

Gremio. – Andrea alone, sitting down.) No money from that Jew! Endless entreaties and no money! What can I say when the King of France's envoys[14]... Oh, Andrea, poor Andrea, how can you even pronounce that word? Piles of money in your hands; the finest mission a king ever entrusted to a man; a hundred masterpieces to bring back, a hundred poor, sick artists to heal and make rich! The role of a guardian angel to play! The nation's blessings to receive and after that, to fill a palace with magnificent works and rekindle the sacred fire of the arts that was ready for extinction in Florence! Andrea, how happily you would have knelt down at your bedside on the day you made a faithful accounting! And King Francis himself is asking you for it! The spotless knight, an honest as well as a generous man! The protector of the arts, the father of an age as beautiful as antiquity![15] He trusted in you and you deceived him! You have robbed him, Andrea, for that is what it is called, make no mistake. Where has that money gone? Jewelry for your wife, parties, entertainments more cheerless than boredom itself. *(He rises.)* Do you realize, Andrea? You are disgraced! Today you are respected, cherished by your pupils, beloved of an angel. Oh, Lucrezia, Lucrezia! Tomorrow, the talk of Florence, for sooner or later those dreaded accounts... Damnation, my wife herself knows nothing of it! Oh, that is what it means to lack character! What harm was *she* doing in asking me for what she liked? And I gave it to her because she asked for it, nothing more. Cursed weakness! Not a single comment. What does honor require, then? And Cordiani? Why didn't I consult him, my best, my only friend, and what will he say? Honor... Am I not an honest man? And yet I have committed a theft. Oh, if it was a question of entering a nobleman's house, breaking open a strong-box and running away—that is horrible to think of, impossible. But when the money is there in your hands, and you have only to dip into it, when poverty hounds you, not for yourself, but for Lucrezia! My sole earthly possession, my sole joy, ten years' love! And then you tell yourself that after all, with a little work, you can replace... Oh yes, replace! The porch of the Annunciation church[16] earned me a sack of wheat!

Gremio *(returning.)* That's done, now. We can leave when you want.

Andrea What is the matter, Gremio? I was watching you put on the bridles. You are using your left hand today.

Gremio My left... Oh, oh, I know what it is. Please your Excellency, my right arm is a bit wounded. Oh, nothing special, but I am getting old and, well, when I was younger... I would have said...

Andrea You say you have been wounded? Who did it?

Gremio Ah, there's the rub! Who? Nobody, and yet I have been wounded. Oh, that's not to say that I can complain, in all conscience...

Andrea No one? Yourself, evidently.

Gremio Oh no, oh no, it wouldn't be so funny, otherwise. No one, least of all myself.

Andrea If you are joking, this is the wrong time for it. Let us get back in the saddle and leave.

Gremio Amen! What I was saying wasn't meant to anger you, and even less as a joke. *He* wasn't laughing very much this morning, when he ran by me and gave it to me.

Andrea Who? What do you mean? Who gave it to you? You are acting very strangely, Gremio.

Gremio Well, then, in faith, listen. You're my master. There are no two ways about it, this must be known. And who is to know it, if not you? Here is the story: I heard someone walking in the courtyard, around four this morning. I got up and I saw a man in a cloak slipping silently down from the window.

Andrea What window?

Gremio A man in a cloak, so I shouted at him to stop. Naturally, I thought it was a robber. Well, instead of stopping, you can see by my arm, it was his dagger that scratched me.

Andrea What window, Gremio?

Gremio Oh, that's another thing. Well, listen, since I have started, it was Miz Lucrezia's window.

Andrea Lucrezia's?

Gremio Yes, sir.

Andrea That is strange!

Gremio To make a long story short, he ran into the park. I shouted and I yelled, "Stop, thief!", but that's the funny part: Mister Damian appeared and told me I was wrong, and he knew better than I did. To cap it all, he gave me a purse so I would shut up.

Andrea Damian?

Gremio Yes, sir, here it is. He even...

Andrea From Lucrezia's window? So Damian had seen the man?

Gremio No, sir. He came out as I was yelling.

Andrea What was he like?

Gremio Who? Mister Damian?

Andrea No, the other man.

Gremio Oh, you know, I hardly saw him.

Andrea Tall, or short?

Gremio Neither one. So then, in the morning, you know...

Andrea That is odd. So Damian told you not to mention it?

Gremio At the risk of being dismissed by you.

Andrea By me? Listen, Gremio: tonight when I go to bed, you stay under that window; but you will have to hide, you understand? Take your sword and if anyone should try to... do you get my meaning? Call out loud, don't let yourself be intimidated, I shall be there.

Gremio Yes, sir.

Andrea I would ask someone else than you to do it. But you see, Gremio, I think I know what it is. It is nothing important, you see: a trifle, some young man's joke. Did you see the color of that cloak?

Gremio Black, black..., yes, at least I think so.

Andrea I shall speak to Cordiani about it. All right, then, it is agreed. Tonight around eleven or twelve o'clock. Don't be afraid, I tell you, it is just a joke. You did very well to tell me about it and I wouldn't want anyone else but you to know of this. That is why I am asking you to... —And you didn't see his face?

Gremio Yes, I did. But he ran away so quickly! And then, that dagger-blow...

Andrea He didn't speak?

Gremio A couple of words, a couple of words.

Andrea You didn't recognize the voice?

Gremio Maybe... I don't know. The whole thing took only a second.

Andrea It is incredible! Come along, then. Let's leave right away. Around eleven. I have to speak with Cordiani about it. You are sure which window it was?

Gremio Oh, quite sure.

Andrea Come on, let's go! *(Exeunt.)*

Scene 3.

(Lucrezia, Spinetta.)

Lucrezia Did you leave the door ajar, Spinetta? Did you put the lamp in the stairway?

Spinetta I did everything you told me.

Lucrezia You can put my night-clothes on that chair and leave me alone, my dear child.

Spinetta Yes, Ma'am.

Lucrezia *(at her prie-dieu)* Oh God, why have you entrusted me with another's happiness? If it had been just mine, I would not have defended it, I would not have struggled with you for my life. Why have you trusted me with his?

Spinetta Won't you ever stop praying and weeping this way, my dear mistress? Your eyes are swollen with tears and these past two days you have not taken a moment's rest.

Lucrezia *(praying)* Have I accomplished your fateful mission? Have I saved his soul by damning myself for his sake? If your bleeding arms were not nailed to this crucifix, Jesus, would you open them for me?

Spinetta I cannot leave. How can I leave you alone, the way I see you?

Lucrezia Will you punish him for my sin? He is not the guilty one. He has pronounced no earthly vows. He has not betrayed his wife. He has no duties, no family. He has done nothing but love and be loved.

Spinetta It is almost eleven.

Lucrezia Oh, Spinetta, don't leave me alone! Do my tears distress you, my child? And yet they have to flow. Do you think a person can lose all peace and happiness without suffering? You can read my heart as you do your own, my life is an open book to you and you have read every page of it. Do you think that one can see ten years' calm and innocence fly away without regret?

Spinetta How I pity you!

Lucrezia Loosen my dress. It is eleven o'clock. Give me some water so I can wipe my eyes. He will be here soon, Spinetta! Is my hair undone? Am I too pale? It was mad of me to have wept! My guitar! Set that song in front of me, the one he wrote. He is coming, he is coming, my dear! Am I beautiful tonight? Will he like me this way?

Maid *(entering)* His Lordship Andrea has just come into the apartment. He would like to know if it is all right to enter.

Andrea *(entering)* Good evening, Lucrezia. I know you were not expecting me at so late an hour. All I hope is that I am not troubling you. I pray you, tell me if you were about to send your women off. I shall wait until supper time to see you.

Lucrezia No, no, not yet, truly!

Andrea The moments we spend together are so rare, and they are so dear to me! You alone in all the world console me for the worries that beset me, Lucrezia. Oh, if I were to lose you! All my courage, all my philosophy is there in your eyes. *(He goes to the window and raises the curtain.—Aside)* Gremio is down there, I can see him.

Lucrezia Is there something making you sad, my dear? You seemed joyful at dinner time.

Andrea Joy may sometimes be sad, and melancholy can have a smile on its lips.

Lucrezia Did you go to the farm? By the way, a letter came for you. The King of France's envoys will be coming tomorrow.

Andrea Tomorrow? They are coming tomorrow?

Lucrezia Does that come as bad news for you? Then we could say you are away from Florence, or ill; one way or the other, they would not see you.

Andrea Why not? I shall greet them with pleasure. Am I not ready to settle my accounts? Tell me, Lucrezia: you do like this house? You are often invited out, aren't you? Does the winter seem pleasant to you this year? What shall we do? Do your new jewels suit you? *(A muffled cry is heard in the garden, and rapid footsteps.)* What is the meaning of that noise? What is wrong? *(Cordiani enters the room, completely disheveled.)* What is the matter, Cordiani? What brings you here? What is the meaning of this disorder? What has happened to you? You are as pale as death!

Lucrezia Oh, I am done for!

Andrea Answer me, what brings you at such an hour? Do you have a duel? Do you need me as a second? Have you gambled away your money? Do you want my purse? *(He takes his hand.)* In Heaven's name, speak. You are like a statue.

Cordiani No..., no..., I just wanted to talk to you... to tell you..., to tell the truth, I wanted..., I don't know...

Andrea What have you done with your sword? By God, something strange is going on inside you. Would you like us to go into this sitting-room? Can't you speak in front of these women? What can I do for you? Answer me, there is nothing I would not do. My friend, my dear friend, can you doubt me?

Cordiani You have guessed it. I have a duel. I cannot speak here. I was looking for you; I came in without knowing why. I was told that... that you were here; and I came... I cannot speak here.

Lionel *(entering)* Master, Gremio has been murdered!

Andrea Who says so? *(Several servants enter the room.)*

Servant Master, Gremio has just been killed. The murderer is in this house. He was seen entering through the back door. *(Cordiani withdraws into the crowd.)*

Andrea To arms! To arms! Take these torches and go through all the rooms. Lock the door from the inside.

Lionel He cannot be far. The blow was struck only a moment ago.

Andrea He is dead? Dead? Where is my sword? Ah, here is one on the wall. *(He goes to take a sword. Looking at his hand)* What is this? That is strange, my hand is soaked in blood. Where did this blood come from?

Lionel Come with us, Master. I promise you, we shall find him.

Andrea Where did I get this blood? My hand is covered with it. Who could I have touched? But the only one I touched was... just now... Go away! Get out of here!

Lionel What is the matter with you, Master? Why send us away?

Andrea Get out! Get out! Leave me alone! All right; I don't want a search to be made of the house, none at all, it is no use, I forbid it. Get out of here, all of you! All of you! Obey me when I speak to you! *(All withdraw in silence. Andrea looks at his hand.)* Covered with blood! The only hand I touched was Cordiani's!

ACT TWO
Scene 1.

The garden.

(Night time, moonlight. Cordiani, a servant.)

Cordiani He wants to speak to me?

Servant Yes, sir, without witnesses. This is the place he indicated to me.

Cordiani Then tell him I am waiting for him. *(Exit the servant. Cordiani sits down on a rock.)*

Damian *(off stage)* Cordiani? Where is Cordiani?

Cordiani So, then, what do you want of me?

Damian I just left Andrea. He knows nothing, at least concerning you. He says he knows perfectly well why Gremio was killed, and he does not accuse anyone of it, least of all you.

Cordiani Is that all you have to tell me?

Damian Yes, it is up to you to decide what you are going to do.

Cordiani In that case, leave me alone. *(He goes and sits down again. Lionel and Cesario walk by.)*

Lionel What do you make of that? He sends us away, doesn't want to hear any more about it, leaves a blow like that unavenged! That poor old man had been working for him since he was a child; I saw him rock him on his knees! Oh, by God, if it were me, there would have been more blood shed than just his!

Damian Still, you are not going to accuse a man like Andrea of cowardice.

Lionel Cowardice or weakness, does it matter what you call it? When I was young, things didn't happen that way. It certainly would not have been hard to find the murderer. And if one doesn't want to dirty one's own hands, by my saint, one always has one's friends.

Cesario As for me, I am leaving this place. This morning will be the last time I've come to the academy. Let others come if they wish, I am going to Pontormo's.

Lionel How can you be so heartless? I would not want to change masters for all the gold in the world.

Cesario Bah, I am not the only one. The studio is in a sorry state. Giulietta won't pose any more. At Pontormo's, there is laughter! They fence, drink, and dance the whole day long. Farewell, Lionel, I shall see you later.

Damien What kind of times are we living in! Oh, my good sir, our poor friend is surely to be pitied. Are you going to have supper with us? *(Exeunt.)*

Cordiani *(alone)* Isn't that Andrea I see over there among those trees? He is looking for something. Now he is drawing closer. Ho, Andrea, over here!

Andrea *(entering)* Are we alone?

Cordiani Yes.

Andrea Do you see this dagger, Cordiani? If I were now to lay you out on the ground with a stroke of my hand and bury you under that tree, there, in this sand your shadow is falling on, no one would have anything to say to me. I have the right and your life is mine.

Cordiani You can do it, my friend, you can do it.

Andrea Do you think my hand would shake? No more than yours did just an hour ago against my dear old Gremio's breast. You see, I know all about it, it was you who killed him. What do you expect now? Do you think I am a coward and don't know how to hold a sword? Are you ready to fight? Isn't that your duty and mine?

Cordiani I shall do as you wish.

Andrea Sit down and listen. I was born poor. The luxury around me comes from an evil source: it was an advance that I misused. I alone, still young, survive from among so many renowned painters of the age of Michelangelo,[17] and I see everything crumbling about me day by day. Rome and Venice are still flourishing; our city is no longer anything now. I struggle in vain against the darkness. The sacred torch is dying out in my hand. Do you think it is nothing for a man who has lived by his art for twenty years to see it fall? My studios are deserted, my reputation is gone. I have no children, no hope left to bind me to life. My health is weak and the winds of plague blowing from the Orient make me tremble like a leaf. Tell me, what did I have left in the world? Just suppose that I should happen to place a dagger against my heart during my sleepless nights. Tell me, who has stopped me up to now?

Cordiani Do not go on, Andrea.

Andrea I loved her with an indefinable love. For her I would have fought an army. I would have hoed the soil and dragged the plow to add one more pearl to her hair. The theft I have committed, the advance made by the King of France that they are coming to ask me for tomorrow,[18] and which I no longer have, was for her: if I spent it all, it was to give her a year of riches and happiness, for once in my life to see her surrounded by amusements and parties. My life meant less to me than my honor, and honor less than Lucrezia's love—what am I saying, less than a smile on her lips, a glint of joy in her eyes! What you see here, Cordiani, the abject, suffering creature standing before you, whom you have seen wandering through these dark porticos for ten years, is not Andrea del Sarto. It is a demented creature, open to scorn, to overwhelming anxiety. At my beautiful Lucrezia's feet there was another Andrea, young and happy, carefree as the wind, free and joyous as a bird in flight, Andrea's angel, the soul of this lifeless body that walks around among men. Do you realize now what you have done?

Cordiani Yes, now I do.

Andrea You have killed that man, Cordiani. That man will go to the cemetery tomorrow with old Gremio's remains. The other one will be left behind and he is the one speaking to you here.

Cordiani *(weeping)* Andrea! Andrea!

Andrea Are you weeping for me or for yourself? I have a favor to ask of you. Thank God, there was no scandal last night. Thank God, I saw lightning strike my twenty years of labor without uttering a complaint, without crying out. If my dishonor were public, either I would have killed you or we would go fight a duel tomorrow. As the price of happiness society grants vengeance, and the right to use this *(throwing away his dagger)* has to replace everything for a man who has lost everything. That is the justice of men; and it is not even certain it would not be you they would pity, if you were to die by my hand.

Cordiani What do you want me to do?

Andrea If you have understood what I have said, you realize that I saw neither an odious crime nor a sacred friendship trampled under foot here. I saw nothing but a slash of the scissors to the only thread that binds me to life. I prefer not to think of the hand that did it. The man I am speaking to has no name for me. I am speaking to the murderer of my honor, my love, and my repose. Can the wound he has inflicted in me be healed? Can eternal separation, deathly silence (for he must realize that his life was in my hands), renewed efforts on my part, a fresh attempt to gain control of my life, still be successful? In a word, let him depart, let him be stricken from the book of life for me; let a guilty passion, which cannot have existed without remorse, be broken off forever; let its memory gradually die away, in a year, perhaps two years, and then I, Andrea, will come back, like a plowman ruined by lightning, to rebuild my thatched hut on my devastated field.

Cordiani Oh, my God!

Andrea I have become used to patience. To make that woman love me, for years I followed her shadow over the earth. The ground she walks on is accustomed to the sweat of my brow. Having reached the end of my course, I shall start my work over again. Who knows what may come of a woman's frailty? Who knows how far the inconstancy of those shifting sands can go and whether twenty more years of love and unlimited devotion may not achieve as much as one night of debauchery? For Lucrezia's guilt dates only from today, since it is today that I found your door closed for the first time since you have been in Florence.

Cordiani That is true.

Andrea You are surprised to see I have this much courage, aren't you? Anyone would be, learning about it one day. I agree with you. It is easier to stab someone with a sword. But I have one great misfortune: I do not believe in the hereafter, and I give you my word that if I do not succeed, the day I am completely sure that my happiness is forever destroyed I shall die, one way or another. Until then, I shall go about my task.

Cordiani When must I leave?

Andrea There is a horse at the gate. I give you one hour. Farewell.

Cordiani Your hand, Andrea, your hand!

Andrea *(coming back)* My hand? To whom? Have I insulted you? Have I called you a false friend, a betrayer of the most sacred oaths? Have I told you, you who are killing me, that I would have chosen you to defend me if what you have done had been done by anyone else? Have I told you that last night I lost anything else but Lucrezia's love? Have I spoken to you of some other sorrow? So to whom do you want me to give my hand?

Cordiani Your hand, Andrea! An eternal farewell, but farewell.

Andrea I cannot. There is blood on yours. *(Exit.)*

Cordiani *(alone, knocking on the door)* Ho! Mathurin!

Mathurin Your Excellency?

Cordiani Take my cloak. Throw everything you find on my table and in my chests together. Quick, make a bundle of them and bring it to me at the garden gate. *(He sits down.)*

Mathurin Are you leaving, sir?

Cordiani Do as I say.

Damian *(entering)* I just met Andrea, who told me you are leaving, Cordiani. How happy I am about your decision! Will it be for some time?

Cordiani I don't know. Ah, Damian, do me a favor and help Mathurin choose what I have to take with me.

Mathurin *(on the doorstep)* Oh, it won't take long!

Damian All you need are the must urgent things. We shall send you the rest wherever you intend to stop. By the way, where are you going?

Cordiani I don't know. Hurry up, Mathurin, hurry up.

Mathurin It will be done right away. *(He carries off a bundle.)*

Damian Now, my friend, farewell.

Cordiani Farewell! Farewell! If this evening you should see... — I mean, if tomorrow or some other day...

Damian Who? What do you want?

Cordiani Nothing, nothing. Farewell, Damian, till we meet again.

Damian Bon voyage! *(He embraces him, then exits.)*

Mathurin All is ready, sir.

Cordiani Thank you, my good fellow. Here, take this for all your services during my stay in this house.

Mathurin Oh, your Excellency!

Cordiani *(still seated)* Everything is ready, isn't it?

Mathurin Yes, sir. Should I accompany you?

Cordiani Certainly. — Mathurin!

Mathurin Your Excellency?

Cordiani I cannot leave, Mathurin.

Mathurin You are not leaving?

Cordiani No. It is impossible, don't you see?

Mathurin Do you need anything else?

Cordiani No, I don't need anything. *(Silence. He rises.)* Pale statues, dear walkways, shady paths, how can I leave now? Deep, dark night, don't you know that I cannot leave? Oh walls that I have climbed over! Earth that I have bloodied! *(He falls back on the bench.)*

Mathurin In Heaven's name, alas, he is dying! Help, help!

Cordiani *(getting up again suddenly)* Do not call! Come with me.

Mathurin That is not our way.

Cordiani Silence! Come with me, I say. You are a dead man if you don't obey. *(He draws him toward the house.)*

Mathurin Where are you going, sir?

Cordiani Don't be frightened. I am delirious. It is nothing. Listen. I only want one quite simple thing. Isn't it time for supper, right now? Your master is seated at his table now, surrounded by his friends, and facing him... In a word, my friend, I do not want to go in. I just want to lean my forehead against the window and see them for a moment. Just one minute, and then we shall leave. *(Exeunt.)*

Scene 2.

A room.

(A table is set. Andrea and Lucrezia, seated.)

Andrea Our friends are very late. You are pale, Lucrezia. That scene must have frightened you.

Lucrezia But Lionel and Damian are here. I do not know what can be keeping them.

Andrea You are not wearing your rings any more? Don't you like them? Oh, I was wrong, here is one that I don't recognize.

Lucrezia Truly, that scene did frighten me. I cannot deny that I am not feeling well.

Andrea Show me that ring, Lucrezia. Was it a present? May I admire it?

Lucrezia *(giving him the ring)* It was a gift from Margaret, my childhood friend.

Andrea That is odd, this is not her monogram! Why ever not? It is a charming bauble, but quite fragile. Oh, my Lord, whatever are you going to say? I broke it as I took it from you.

Lucrezia Is it broken? My ring is broken?

Andrea I am so vexed at my clumsiness. But truly, it is beyond repair.

Lucrezia No matter! Give it back to me as it is.

Andrea What could you want to do with it? The cleverest goldsmith could not fix it. *(He throws it to the floor and crushes it.)*

Lucrezia Do not crush it! I was very fond of it!

Andrea All right, Margaret comes here every day. You can tell her that I broke it and she will give you another one. Have we many people coming this evening? Will our supper be a joyous one?

Lucrezia I was very fond of that ring.

Andrea I also lost a very precious jewel last night. I was very fond of it, too... Won't you answer my question?

Lucrezia Why, we shall have our usual company, I suppose: Lionel, Damian, and Cordiani.

Andrea Cordiani, too!... I am deeply grieved at Gremio's death.

Lucrezia He was like a father to you.

Andrea No matter! No matter! Every day one loses a friend. Is it not quite an ordinary thing to hear people say: so-and-so has died, so-and-so is ruined? We dance and drink all the same. All is nothing but fortune and misfortune.

Lucrezia Here come our guests, I believe. *(Enter Lionel and Damian.)*

Andrea Well, my good friends, let us take our places at table! Do you have some care or trouble in your heart? Now is the time to forget all that. Alas, yes, you probably do have; every man under the sun does. *(They sit down.)*

Lucrezia Why is there an empty place?

Andrea Cordiani has gone to Germany.

Lucrezia Cordiani? Gone!

Andrea Yes. To Germany. God keep him! Come now, my friend Lionel, our youth is in these. *(He points to the goblets.)*

Lionel Speak for me alone, Master. May yours endure for many years, for your friends and our country!

Andrea Young or old, what does that word mean? White hair does not make one old and the hearts of men are ageless.

Lucrezia *(softly)* Damian, is it true he has left?

Damian *(as above)* Quite true.

Lionel The sky looks threatening. This is a bad time for traveling.

Andrea My good friends, I am definitely going to leave this house. My dear Lucrezia finds life in Florence less and less to her taste; and as for me, I never have liked it. As of next month I intend to buy a country home on the banks of the Arno, with some green vines and a modest garden. That is where I want to end my days, as I began them. My pupils won't follow me there. What have I to teach them that they cannot forget? I myself forget things every day and less than I would like, at that. Still, I need to relive the past. What do you think, Lucrezia?

Lionel Are you giving up all your hopes?

Andrea They are giving up on me, rather. Oh, my old friend, hope is like a bugle call: she urges us on to battle and she exalts danger. Everything is so fine, so easy, as long as she echoes in the depths of our hearts! But the day her voice is stilled, the soldier halts and shatters his sword.

Damian What is the matter, Madam? You seem ill.

Lionel Why yes, she is quite pale! We ought to leave.

Lucrezia Spinetta! Go into my room, my dear, and get my smelling salts on my dressing table. Bring them to me. *(Exit Spinetta.)*

Andrea What ever is the matter, Lucrezia? Good Heavens, could you really be ill?

Damian Open the window, the fresh air will do you good. *(Spinetta returns, terrified.)*

Spinetta My lord, my lord! There is a man hiding there.

Andrea Where?

Spinetta There, in my mistress's apartment.

Lionel Death and damnation! That is the result of your weakness, Master. It must be Gremio's murderer. Let me talk to him.

Spinetta I went in without a lamp. He grabbed my hand as I was going between the two doors.

Andrea Lionel, don't go in there. This is my business.

Lionel Even if you should banish me from your house, this time I cannot leave you. Let's go in, Damian. *(Exit.)*

Andrea *(running to his wife)* Is it he, you wretch? Is it he?

Lucrezia O my Lord! Take pity on me! *(She faints.)*

Damian Follow Lionel, Andrea, don't let him see Cordiani.

Andrea Cordiani! Cordiani! Is my dishonor such common knowledge, so evident to all around me, that I only have to say one word for people to answer: Cordiani! Cordiani! *(Shouting.)* Come out now, you wretch, since Damian here is calling you! *(Lionel comes back out with Cordiani.—To everyone:)* I asked you to leave a while ago. Now I pray you to remain here. Take this woman away, gentlemen. This man is Gremio's murderer. *(Lucrezia is carried away.)* He killed him in order to enter my wife's room. A horse!... No matter how she may feel, Damian, you shall take her to her mother's house... this very evening, right this minute. Now Lionel, you are going to be my second. Cordiani can take whomever he wants. For you see what is happening, my friend, don't you?

Lionel My swords are in my room. We can get them on our way out.

Andrea *(to Cordiani)* So, you want my dishonor to be common knowledge! It will be, sir, it will be. But the satisfaction will be, too, and a curse on him who makes it necessary. *(Exeunt.)*

Scene 3.

An open space at one end of the garden.

(A lamp is lit. Mathurin alone, then John.)

Mathurin Where can that young man have gone? He tells me to wait for him and it has been almost half an hour since he left me. How he trembled as he walked toward the house. Oh, if what they say about him was really true!

John *(passing by)* Well, Mathurin, what are you doing here at this hour?

Mathurin I am waiting for master Cordiani.

John Aren't you coming to poor Gremio's funeral? We are going to leave in just a while.

Mathurin Really, I am afraid I can't leave this spot.

John Well, I am going right now.

Mathurin John, do you see those men coming from the house? They look like our master and his friends.

John Yes, indeed, it is them. What the devil are they looking for? They are coming straight toward us.

Mathurin Don't they have swords in their hands?

John I don't think so. Why yes, you're right. It looks like a duel.

Mathurin Let's move off and if I don't hear my name called, I shall go with you. *(Exeunt. Enter Lionel and Cordiani.)*

Lionel This light will do. You stand here, sir. Won't you have a second?

Cordiani No, sir.

Lionel That is not the custom. Let me say for myself that I regret it. When I was young, there never were any affairs of this kind without four swords drawn.

Cordiani This is not a duel, sir. Andrea won't have any need to parry and the fight will not last long.

Lionel What are you saying? Do you want to make him a murderer?

Cordiani I am surprised he isn't here yet.

Andrea *(entering)* Here I am.

Lionel Take off your coats. I shall draw the lines. Gentlemen, you can break as far as this.

Andrea En garde!

Damian *(entering)* I could not carry out the mission you entrusted me with. Lucrezia refuses my escort. She left on foot alone, accompanied by her maid.

Andrea God in heaven! What a storm is brewing! *(Thunder.)*

Damian Lionel, I offer myself as Cordiani's second. Andrea should see nothing in this act but a duty I hold sacred. I shall draw my sword only if I am absolutely obliged to.

Cordiani Thank you, Damian, thank you.

Lionel Are you both ready?

Andrea I am.

Cordiani I am. *(They fence. Cordiani is wounded.)*

Damian Cordiani is wounded!

Andrea *(running to him)* Are you wounded, my friend?

Lionel *(restraining him)* Step back. We shall take care of the rest.

Cordiani It is just a slight wound. I can still hold my sword.

Lionel No, sir, you will be feeling much more pain in a moment. The sword pierced you. If you can walk, come with us.

Cordiani You are right. Are you coming, Damian? Give me your arm, I feel very faint. You can leave me at Manfredi's.

Andrea *(softly, to Lionel)* Do you think it is fatal?

Lionel I cannot vouch for anything. *(Exeunt.)*

Andrea *(alone)* Why are they leaving me? I must go with them. Where do they think I can go? *(He takes a few steps toward the house.)* Ah, that empty house! No, by heaven, I shall not go back in there tonight. If those two bedrooms are to be empty tonight, so shall mine. He did not defend himself. I did not feel his sword. He received the blow, that is clear. He will die at Manfredi's.

It is strange. And yet I have already fought a duel. Lucrezia gone, all alone, on this awful night! Isn't that someone's footsteps I hear over there? *(He goes toward the trees.)*

No, it is no one. He is going to die. Lucrezia alone, with a woman! Well, what of it? I have been deceived by that woman. I fight a duel with her lover. I wound him. Now I have had my revenge. Everything is as it should be. What is there for me to do now?

Oh, that empty house! It is terrible. When I think of what it was like last night, what I had then, what I have lost! What does vengeance mean to me? What, is this all? To be left alone this way? Whose life does it restore to put a murderer to death? What! Answer me! What business did I have to send my wife away, to slaughter that man? There is no offended party, there is just an unhappy man. What do I care about your laws of honor! A fine consolation for you to have invented for men who are in my position, for you to have arranged as a ceremony! Where are my twenty years of happiness, my wife, my friend, the sunshine of my days, the repose of my nights? Here is all that is left to me. *(He looks at his sword.)* What do you want of me? They call you the friend of the offended. Here there is no offended man. Let the morning dew wipe you clean of blood! *(He throws it away.)* Oh, that terrible house! My God! My God! *(He weeps bitter tears.)*

(The funeral passes by.)

Who are you burying there?

Bearers Nicholas Gremio.

Andrea So, my poor old friend, you, too, are abandoning me!

ACT THREE
Scene 1.

A street.

(It is still night-time. Enter Lionel, Damian, and Cordiani.)

Cordiani I cannot walk; the blood is choking me. Let me stop at this bench. *(They put him down on the bench.)*

Lionel How do you feel?

Cordiani I am dying, I am dying! In heaven's name, a glass of water!

Damian You stay here, Lionel. I know a doctor who lives down that street. I shall run and get him.

Cordiani It is too late, Damian.

Lionel Be patient. I shall go and knock on the door of this house. *(He knocks.)* Perhaps we can find some help here until the doctor arrives. No one! *(He knocks again.)*

A voice *(within)* Who is there?

Lionel Open up! Open up, whoever you may be yourself. In the name of hospitality, open up!

Paolo *(opening the door)* What do you want?

Lionel There is a gentleman here who is mortally wounded. Bring us a glass of water and something to dress his wound. *(Exit Paolo.)*

Cordiani Leave me, Lionel. Go get Andrea. He is the one who is wounded, not me. He is the one whom all human science won't heal tonight. Poor Andrea! Poor Andrea!

Paolo *(coming back)* Drink this, my dear lord, and may heaven come to your aid!

Lionel Whose house is this?

Paolo Madonna Flora del Fede's.

Cordiani Lucrezia's mother! Oh, Lionel, Lionel, let's get away from here. *(He rises.)* I cannot move. I have no more strength left.

Lionel Hasn't her daughter Lucrezia been here this evening?

Paolo No, sir.

Lionel No! Not yet! That is strange!

Paolo Why should she come at such an hour? *(Lucrezia and Spinetta arrive.)*

Lucrezia Knock on the door, Spinetta. I don't feel I have the courage to.

Spinetta Who is there on that bench, covered with blood and on the brink of death?

Cordiani Oh, damn it!

Lucrezia You ask who? It is Cordiani. *(She rushes to the bench.)* Is it you? Is it you? Who brought you here? Who left you alone on this stone? Where is Andrea, Lionel? Oh, he is dying! Paolo, why haven't you had him taken into my mother's house?

Paolo My mistress is not in Florence, Ma'am.

Lucrezia Where is she, then? Are there no doctors in Florence? Come, sir, help me, and let us carry him into the house.

Spinetta Think what you are doing, Ma'am.

Lucrezia Think of what? Are you mad? What does it matter? Can't you see that he is dying? I would do it even if it wasn't him. *(Damian and a doctor arrive.)*

Damian This way, sir. Please God we are in time!

Lucrezia *(to the doctor)* Come, sir, help us. Open up the doors, Paolo. It isn't fatal, is it?

Damian Wouldn't it be better to try and carry him to Manfredi's?

Lucrezia Who is Manfredi? I am here, I am his mistress. This is my house. He is dying for me, isn't he? Well, then, what have you to say? Yes, of course I am Andrea del Sarto's wife. What do I care what people will say? Haven't I been sent away by my husband? Won't I be the talk of the city two hours from now? Manfredi? And what can people say? They will say that Lucrezia del Fede found Cordiani dying at her door and she had him taken into her house. Come in, come in! *(They go into the house, carrying Cordiani.)*

Lionel *(remaining alone)* My duty has been done. Now let us see about Andrea! The poor man must be deeply grieved! *(Enter Andrea, pensive, and goes toward the house.)* Who are you? Where are you going? *(Andrea does not reply.)* Is that you, Andrea? Why have you come?

Andrea I am going to see my wife's mother.

Lionel She is not in Florence.

Andrea Ah! Then where is Lucrezia, in that case?

Lionel I do not know. But what I am certain of is that Madonna Flora is away. Go back home, my friend.

Andrea How do you know that and how do you happen to be here?

Lionel I was coming back from Manfredi's, where I left Cordiani, and as I passed by I decided to find out...

Andrea Cordiani is dying, isn't he?

Lionel No, his friends hope that he can be saved.

Andrea You are wrong, there are people in the house. Just look at the lights going back and forth. *(He goes and looks in a window.)* Ah!

Lionel What do you see?

Andrea Am I mad, Lionel? I thought I saw Cordiani go by in the downstairs room, covered with blood, leaning on Lucrezia's arm.

Lionel You saw Cordiani leaning on Lucrezia's arm?

Andrea Soaked in his own blood.

Lionel Let us go back to your house, my friend.

Andrea Be still! I have to knock on the door.

Lionel What for? I tell you Madonna Flora is away. I just knocked on it myself.

Andrea I saw him! Let me be.

Lionel What are you going to do, my friend? Are you a man? If your wife has so little self-respect as to welcome the author of a crime you have punished into her mother's house, is it right for you to forget that he is dying by your hand and disturb his last moments?

Andrea What do you want me to do? Yes, yes, I could kill them both! Oh, I have lost my senses! I am seeing things that don't exist. This entire night I have run around through these deserted streets, surrounded by hideous phantoms. Look here, I have bought poison.

Lionel Lean on my arm and let us go.

Andrea *(returning to the window)* Nothing! They are in there, aren't they?

Lionel In the name of God, get hold of yourself. What do you want to do? It is impossible for you to witness such a scene and any violence on this occasion would be cruelty. Your enemy is dying. What more do you want?

Andrea My enemy! Him, my enemy! My dearest and best friend? What has he done, then? He loved her. Let us go, Lionel, I could kill them both with my own hands.

Lionel We shall see tomorrow what is left for you to do. Trust in me; your honor is as sacred to me as my own, my gray hair is an earnest of that.

Andrea What is left for me to do? What do you think will become of me? I have to speak to Lucrezia. *(He walks toward the door.)*

Lionel Andrea, Andrea, I beg of you, don't go near that door. Have you lost any sort of courage? The position you are in is terrible, no one sympathizes more keenly, more sincerely than I. I have a wife, too, I have children. But shouldn't a man's steadfastness serve as his shield? Tomorrow you will be able to listen to advice that I cannot give you right now.

Andrea It is true, it is true! Let him die in peace, in her arms, Lionel! She is watching and weeping over him! Through the shadows of death, he can see that beloved face moving about him. She smiles at him and encourages him! She offers him a health-giving draught; for him she is the image of life. Oh, all that once was mine! That was how I wanted to die. Come, let us go, Lionel. *(He knocks on the door.)* Ho, Paolo! Paolo!

Lionel What are you doing, wretch?

Andrea I won't go in. *(Paolo appears.)* Put your lamp down on this bench. I have to write to Lucrezia.

Lionel And what do you want to say to her?

Andrea Here, give this note to her. Tell her that I shall await her reply at my house. Yes, at my house. I can't stay here. Come, Lionel. At my house, do you understand? *(Exeunt.)*

Scene 2.

Andrea's house.

(Daylight. John, Montjoie.)

John I think someone is knocking at the gate. *(He opens.)* What do you want, your Excellency? *(Enter Montjoie and his retinue.)*

Montjoie The painter Andrea del Sarto?

John He is not at home, my lord.

Montjoie If his door is shut, tell him that the King of France's envoy is asking for him.

John If your Excellency will be so kind as to go into the academy, my master may be back any time now.

Montjoie Let us go in, gentlemen. I must say I don't mind visiting the studios and seeing his pupils.

John Alas, my lord, the academy is empty today! My master has taken very few pupils this year and starting today no one will come here any more.

Montjoie Really? I had been told just the opposite... Doesn't your master teach in the school any longer?

John Here he comes himself, accompanied by one of his friends.

Montjoie Who, that man who is coming around the corner? The old or the young one?

John The younger of the two.

Montjoie How pale and weary his face looks! What profound sadness is written all over his features! Is that the painter Andrea del Sarto? *(Enter Andrea and Lionel.)*

Lionel I greet your lordship. Who are you?

Montjoie Our business is with Andrea del Sarto. I am Count de Montjoie, the King of France's envoy.

Andrea The King of France? I have robbed your master, sir. The money he entrusted me with has been wasted and I have not bought a single painting for him. *(To a servant.)* Has Paolo come?

Montjoie Are you serious?

Lionel Do not believe him, gentlemen. My friend Andrea... for certain reasons... an unfortunate affair... is in no condition to answer you and to have the honor of your visit today.

Montjoie If that is the way it is, we shall come back another day.

Andrea Why? I tell you I have robbed him. That is a very serious matter. You didn't know that I robbed him, Lionel? It would be the same thing even if you were to come back a hundred times.

Montjoie That is incredible.

Andrea Not at all. It is quite simple. I had a wife... No, no! I just mean that I have made use of the King of France's money as if it were my own.

Montjoie Is that how you carry out your promises? Where are the pictures that Francis the First commissioned you to buy for him?

Andrea Mine are in there. Take them if you like. They are worthless. I once had genius, or something resembling genius; but I always painted my pictures too quickly, in order to get cash. Take them anyway. John, bring the two pictures that you find on the easel. My wife loved pleasure, gentlemen. You can tell the King of France to demand extradition and he can have me tried by his courts. Ah, Correggio, there is a painter! He used to be poorer than I, but a painting never left his studio a quarter-hour too soon. Honesty! Honesty! That is the watchword. Women's hearts are an abyss.

Montjoie *(to Lionel)* His words foretell delirium. What should we make of this? Is this the man who lived like a prince in the court of France?[19] Everyone heeded his advice like an oracle's when it came to architecture and the arts.

Lionel I cannot tell you the cause of the state you see him in. If you are moved by it, treat him gently. *(The two paintings are brought in.)*

Andrea Ah, here they are. Well, gentlemen, have them taken with you. Not that I attribute any value to them. Such a large sum, in any case, enough to buy Raphaels with! Ah, Raphael! He died a happy man, in the arms of his mistress.

Montjoie *(looking at one of them)* This is a magnificent painting!

Andrea Too quick! Too quick! Take them away. Let it all be over. Ah, wait a moment. *(He stops the porters.)* You are looking at me, poor girl! *(To the face of Charity represented in the picture.)* You want to bid me farewell! This was Charity,[20] gentlemen. This was the most beautiful, the gentlest of human virtues. You had no model, no! You appeared to me in a vision one gloomy night, pale as you are here, surrounded by your dear children, who suck your breast! This one has just fallen to the ground and gazes at his beautiful nurturing spirit while gathering a few wildflowers. Give this to your master, gentlemen. My name is at the bottom. That is worth some money. Paolo hasn't come to ask for me?

Servant No, sir.

Andrea What in the world can he be doing? My life is in his hands.

Lionel *(to Montjoie)* In heaven's name, gentlemen, please go! I shall bring him to you tomorrow, if I can. You can see for yourself, an unexpected misfortune has clouded his mind.

Montjoie We shall obey, sir. Excuse us, but don't forget your promise. *(Exeunt.)*

Andrea I was born to live in peace, don't you see! I am not good at unhappiness. What can be keeping Paolo?

Lionel What did you ask in that damned letter, whose reply you are awaiting so impatiently?

Andrea You are right. Let us go there ourselves. It is always better to have things out in person.

Lionel Don't go off right now. Paolo is supposed to meet you here. It would just be a waste of time.

Andrea She won't reply. That is the supreme abjection! I beg, Lionel, when I ought to be punishing. Do not judge me as you might some other man, my friend. I am a man without character,[21] don't you see? I was born to live in peace.

Lionel His grief appalls me despite myself.

Andrea Oh, what shame! What humiliation! She won't reply. How did I come to this? Do you know what I asked her to do? Oh, cowardice itself would blush, Lionel. I ask her to come back to me.

Lionel Is that possible?

Andrea Yes, yes, I know all that. I made a scandal. Well, tell me, what did I gain by it? I acted as you wished. Well, I am the most unhappy of men. Let me tell you, then, I love her, I love her more than ever!

Lionel You madman!

Andrea Do you think she will agree? You have to pardon me for being a coward. My father was just a poor workman.[22] Paolo won't come. I am not a gentleman; the blood flowing in my veins is not noble blood.

Lionel More noble than you realize.

Andrea My father was a poor workman... Do you think Cordiani will die? The little talent that people saw in me made the poor man think I was protected by a fairy godmother. And I would gaze at the woods and the streams during my walks, always hoping to see my divine protectress come forth from some mysterious grotto. That is how all-powerful nature drew me to herself. I learned painting and, bit by bit, the veil of illusions crumbled into dust at my feet.

Lionel Poor Andrea!

Andrea She alone!—yes, when she appeared, I thought my dream was coming true and that my Galatæa was being brought to life in my hands. What a madman! My genius died in my love. All was lost for me... Cordiani is dying and Lucrezia will try and follow him... Ah, hell and damnation, that man will not come.

Lionel Send someone to Madonna Flora's house.

Andrea That is true. Mathurin, go to Madonna Flora's house. Listen. *(Aside.)* Keep your eyes open; try and prowl around the house; ask for the answer to my letter; go, and come back right away... But why not ourselves, Lionel? Oh, solitude, solitude! What shall I do with these hands?

Lionel Calm yourself, I beg you.

Andrea I would hold her in my arms during the long summer nights on my gothic balcony. I watched the stars of blighted worlds falling in silence. What is glory, I would cry, what is ambition? Alas, men hold out to nature a cup as broad and as empty as herself. She lets just one drop of her dew fall into it; but that drop is love, it is a tear from her eye, the only one she has shed on this earth to console it for having issued forth from her hands. Lionel, Lionel, my hour has come.

Lionel Take courage.

Andrea It is strange, I never felt this way before. It seemed to me as if a blow struck me. Everything is separating itself from me. It seemed to me that Lucrezia was leaving.

Lionel That Lucrezia was leaving!

Andrea Yes, I am sure that Lucrezia is leaving without answering me.

Lionel How could that be?

Andrea I am sure of it. I just saw her.

Lionel Saw her! Where? How?

Andrea I am sure of it. She is gone.

Lionel That is strange!

Andrea Look, here comes Mathurin.

Mathurin *(entering)* Is my master here?

Andrea Yes, here I am.

Mathurin I found out everything.

Andrea Well?

Mathurin *(drawing him aside)* Should I tell you everything, master?

Andrea Yes, yes.

Mathurin I prowled around the house as you ordered me to.

Andrea Well?

Mathurin I got the old doorkeeper talking, so I know absolutely everything.

Andrea Go ahead, speak.

Mathurin Cordiani is better. The wound was nothing much. He was relieved by a single cut of the scalpel.

Andrea And Lucrezia?

Mathurin She has gone with him.

Andrea Who do you mean, *him*?

Mathurin Cordiani.

Andrea You are crazy. A man I saw about to give up the ghost, just... it was this very evening.

Mathurin He insisted on leaving as soon as he felt strong enough to walk. He said that a soldier would do as much in his place and that he had to choose either life or death.

Andrea That is incredible! Where are they going?

Mathurin They have set out for Piedmont.

Andrea Both of them on horseback!

Mathurin Yes, sir.

Andrea That is not possible. He couldn't walk last night.

Mathurin Still, it is true. Paolo, the gatekeeper, told me the whole thing.

Andrea Lionel! Did you hear, Lionel! They are leaving together for Piedmont.

Lionel What is that you say, Andrea?

Andrea Nothing, nothing! Saddle a horse! Quickly, come on, I have to leave right away. I may as well go myself. Which gate did they leave by?

Mathurin The one by the river.

Andrea Good, good! My cloak! Farewell, Lionel.

Lionel Where are you going?

Andrea I don't know, I don't know! Ah, weapons! Blood!

Lionel Where are you going? Answer me!

Andrea As for the King of France, I have robbed him. Even if I were to go and see them tomorrow, it would still be the same thing. So... *(He meets Damian as he is going out.)*

Damian Where are you going, Andrea?

Andrea Ah, you are right. The ground is wavering. Oh, Damian, Damian! *(He falls in a faint.)*

Lionel This past night has killed him. I could not bear his ill fortune.

Damian Let me moisten his temples. *(He dips his handkerchief into a fountain.)* My poor friend! How one night has changed him! Look, he is opening his eyes again.

Andrea Have they gone, Damian?

Damian What can I say to him? Has he found everything out, then?

Andrea Do not lie to me. I shall not pursue them. I have no strength left. What did I think I could do? I tried to be brave and I am not. Now, as you can see, I cannot leave. Let me speak to this man.

Mathurin *(drawing near Andrea)* What do you want, master?

Andrea Am I not dishonored, anyway? What is left for me to do in this world? Oh, light of the sun! Oh, beauteous nature! They are in love, they are happy. How joyously they are riding over the plain! Their horses go faster and the passing wind carries off their kisses. The fatherland? The fatherland? Those who run off together have none.

Damian His hand is as cold as marble.

Andrea *(softly, to Mathurin)* Listen to me, Mathurin, listen to me and remember my words. You will take a horse; you will go to Madonna Flora's house and get precise information on their route. You will set off at a galop. Remember what I am telling you. Don't make me say it again, I couldn't. You will catch up with them on the plain. You will greet them, Mathurin, and tell them: "Why are you fleeing so swiftly? Andrea del Sarto's widow can marry Cordiani."

Mathurin Must I say that, my lord?

Andrea Go, go, don't make me say it again. *(Exit Mathurin.)*

Lionel What did you tell that man?

Andrea Do not stop him. He is going to my mother-in-law's house. Now, have them bring me my cup, full of strong wine.

Lionel He can barely stand up.

Andrea Take me as far as the door, my friends. *(Raising the cup.)* This was the one I used in our joyous festivities.

Damian What are you looking for in your breast pocket?

Andrea Nothing, nothing! I thought I had lost it. *(He drinks.)* To the death of the arts in Italy!

Lionel Stop. What is in that flask that you poured a few drops from and then let fall from your hand?

Andrea It is a powerful draught. Bring it up to your lips and you will be cured of whatever illness you suffer from. *(He dies.)*

Scene 3.

Woods and mountains.

(Lucrezia and Cordiani on a hill, with their horses in the rear.)

Cordiani Come, the sun is going down. It is time to get back on our horses.

Lucrezia My horse reared up as we left the city! In truth, all these sinister omens are quite strange.

Cordiani I don't want to have time either to think or to suffer. I am wearing a double bandage on my double wound. Let us go on, let us not wait for night to fall.

Lucrezia Who is that rider racing up at full speed? I have seen him behind us for quite a while.

Cordiani Let us get onto our horses again, Lucrezia, and not look back.

Lucrezia He is coming closer! He is getting off near me.

Cordiani Let us go! Get up and do not listen to him. *(They walk toward their horses.)*

Mathurin *(getting off his horse)* Why are you fleeing so swiftly? Andrea del Sarto's widow can marry Cordiani.

End

Lorenzaccio

By any standard, *Lorenzaccio* represents a major literary achievement. It is certainly one of the longest, most complex historical dramas ever written (Victor Hugo's *Cromwell* remaining *hors concours...*). Its thirty-five characters and thirty-eight scenes, involving three major plots and numerous sub-plots, ought to make it a formless "slice of history." But, in fact, it is a remarkably tight and well-constructed play, whose principal drawback was that it was not at all adapted to the stage resources of its times. That no doubt explains why it was not produced during its author's lifetime; indeed, not at all until 1896, almost forty years after Musset's death. Even then it was reduced to a disfigured, truncated form commissioned by Sarah Bernhardt so that she might add Lorenzo to her list of travesty roles, which also included Hamlet. Following a series of more or less complete stagings, usually with a female actress—Falconetti, Marie-Thérèse Piérat, Marguerite Jamois—as the protagonist, the first integral presentation of the play with a male actor in the title role had to wait for Jean Vilar's 1952 production in Paris, starring Gérard Philipe, at the *Théâtre national populaire*.

Recent information on the origins of the play indicates that it was written practically in its entirety before Musset's voyage to Italy in 1833-1834 with his lover, George Sand, elaborating on a *scène historique* that she had written, perhaps in collaboration with an earlier lover, Jules Sandeau.[1] Any "local color" is thus due more to the poet's imagination and his historical sources than to first-hand experience of Florence and Venice. Although Musset apparently considered publishing it, like most of his dramatic work, in the *Revue des deux mondes*, it first saw print in 1834 in the second "*livraison*" of *Un Spectacle dans un fauteuil*. Despite the speed of its writing—particularly when one considers its generous dimensions—*Lorenzaccio* evidently caused Musset a good deal of concern. Paul Dimoff published three complete sets of plans for the drama, as well as two fully-developed scenes that Musset decided not to use in its final version. Interestingly enough, both of these involve artists—the fictional Tebaldeo

Freccia, to whom I have referred in the general introduction to this volume, and a historical figure, Benvenuto Cellini—and thus confirm, in my opinion, Musset's desire to avoid any redemptive artistic theme for his play. Rather, the "message" carried by it is the impossibility of meaningful or "pure" political action, in the face of internal and external forces that alter and corrupt human motivation.

Cast of Characters:

Alessandro de' Medici	the Duke of Florence[2]
Lorenzo de' Medici ("Lorenzaccio"),[3]	the Duke's cousin
Cosimo de' Medici	another cousin of the Duke
Cardinal Cibo[4]	
Marquis Cibo	his brother[5]
Ascanio	the Marquis' son
Lord Maurizio	the Chancellor of the Council of Eight
Cardinal Baccio[6] *Valori*	the Pope's representative
Giuliano Salviati	
Filippo Strozzi[7]	
Piero Strozzi	his son
Tommaso Strozzi	another son of Filippo
Leone Strozzi	another son, Prior of Capua
Roberto Corsini	the Governor of the fortress of Florence
Palla Ruccellai[8]	nobleman in favor of a republic
Alamanno Salviati	other nobleman in favor of a republic
Francesco Pazzi	other nobleman in favor of a republic
Bindo Altoviti	Lorenzo's uncle
Battista Venturi	a burgher
Tebaldeo Freccia	a painter[9]
Scoronconcolo[10]	a hired killer

The Council of Eight	
Giomo [the Hungarian][11]	the Duke's squire
Maffio	a burgher
Agnolo	Marquise Cibo's page
Maria Soderini[12]	Lorenzo's mother
Caterina Ginori	his aunt[13]
Marquise Ricciarda Cibo	[Marquis Cibo's wife]
Luisa Strozzi	[Filippo Strozzi's daughter]

Two ladies of the Court and a German officer, a goldsmith, a merchant, two tutors and two children, pages, soldiers, monks, courtiers, exiles, schoolboys, servants, burghers, etc.

Florence[14]
ACT ONE
Scene 1.

A garden.

(Moonlight; one wing of a house in the rear, another toward the front. Enter Duke Alessandro and Lorenzo, wrapped in their cloaks, and Giomo, with a lantern in his hand.)

Duke If we have to wait another fifteen minutes, I'll leave. It is as cold as the devil.

Lorenzo Patience, your Highness, patience.

Duke She was supposed to leave her mother's apartments at midnight. It is midnight now and still she has not come.

Lorenzo If she does not come, you can call me a fool and the old mother a virtuous woman.

Duke By the Pope's guts! To top it all, I have been robbed of a thousand ducats!

Lorenzo We only put up half of it in advance. I can answer for the young minx. Those two great languid eyes just don't lie. Is there anything more interesting for a connoisseur than corrupting a suckling child? Sensing the future bawd in a fifteen-year-old girl; planning, sowing, paternally insinuating an intricate strain of depravity while giving some friendly advice and fondling her chin; —saying everything, or nothing, according to the parents' nature;—gradually accustoming the nascent imagination to give shape to its fantasies, to touch what frightens her, to scorn what protects her! It goes more quickly than you would think. The important thing is to strike just right. And what a treasure this one is! Just what your Highness needs to spend a delightful night! Such modesty! A young kitten that would like to have some jam but doesn't want to get her paws dirty. Tidy as a Dutchwoman! The very embodiment of bourgeois mediocrity. Besides, she is the daughter of fine people whose lack of wealth has not allowed a solid education. There is no base to their morals, nothing but a thin veneer. But what a violent flood, a prodigious torrent, beneath that slim layer of ice, which cracks at each step! Never has a flowering shrub promised daintier fruits; never have I sensed in a childish aura a more exquisite odor of debauchery.

Duke 'Sblood! I don't see the signal. But I have to go to Nasi's ball: he is marrying off his daughter today.

Giomo Let us go up to the house, my lord. Since it is just a matter of carrying off a girl who is already half paid-for, we can certainly go and rap on the window.

Duke Come over this way, Giomo is right. *(They go off. Enter Maffio.)*

Maffio In my dream, I thought I saw my sister walking through our garden holding a darkened lantern and covered with jewels. I awoke with a start. God knows it was just an illusion, but too strong an illusion for sleep not to have fled before it. Thank heaven the windows of the wing where the girl sleeps are shut, as usual. I can just make out the light of her lamp amid the leaves of our old fig tree. Now my wild fears are evaporating; the rapid beating of my heart gives way to gentle peace. Madman! my eyes are welling up with tears, as if my poor sister had faced real danger.—What is that I hear? Who is moving among the branches? *(Maffio's sister passes in the distance.)* Am I awake? It is the ghost of my sister. It is holding a darkened lantern and a shining necklace is sparkling on her breast in the rays of the moon. Gabriella! Gabriella! Where are you going? *(Giomo and the Duke come back on stage.)*

Giomo That must be her little old brother, walking in his sleep.— Lorenzo will take your beauty to the palace by the back door. As for us, what have we to fear?

Maffio Who are you? Ho! Stop! *(He draws his sword.)*

Giomo My dear bumpkin, we are your friends.

Maffio Where is my sister? What are you doing here?

Giomo Your sister has flown the coop, my good peasant. Open up your garden gate.

Maffio Draw your sword and defend yourself, you murderer!

Giomo *(seizing him and disarming him)* Stand back! Not so fast, you fool!

Maffio Oh, the shame! This is too much! If there are any laws in Florence, if some kind of justice remains alive on earth, by all that is truest and most sacred in the world I shall throw myself at the Duke's feet and he will have you both hanged.

Giomo At the Duke's feet?

Maffio Yes, yes, I know that scoundrels of your kind slaughter families with impunity. But if I am to die, do you hear, I shall not die in silence like so many others. If the Duke does not know that his city is a forest infested with bandits, full of poisoners and dishonored girls, I am one man who will say it to him. Ah, murder, ah, blood and thunder, I shall get justice from you.

Giomo *(with his sword in his hand)* Should I strike him, your Highness?

Duke Come now! Strike this man!? Go back to bed, my friend. We shall send you a few ducats tomorrow. *(Exit.)*

Maffio That was Alessandro de' Medici!

Giomo In person, my good bumpkin. Don't brag about his visit, though, if you want to hang on to your ears. *(Exit.)*

Scene 2.

A street.

(Daybreak. Several masked persons come out of a brightly lit house. A silk merchant and a goldsmith[15] *open up their shops.)*

Merchant Ho, ho, Mondella, old friend, there's a lot of wind for my cloth. *(He displays bolts of silk.)*

Goldsmith *(yawning)* They could split your head open. The devil take their revelry! I didn't shut an eye all night.

Merchant My wife didn't, either, neighbor. The dear soul turned over and over like an eel. Oh, well, when you are young, you don't go to sleep at the sound of music.

Goldsmith Young! Young! That is fine for you to say! You are not young when you have a beard like this; but God knows if their damned music makes me feel like dancing. *(Two schoolboys pass by.)*

First sch. There is no better fun. You slip into the doorway amid the soldiers and you can watch them come down the stairs in costumes of every color. Look, there is the Nasi's house. *(He breathes on his fingers.)* My hands are freezing, holding this portfolio.

Second sch. Will they let us get closer?

First sch. In whose name could they stop us? We are citizens of Florence. Look at all the people around the door. What a lot of horses! And those pages and liveries! They are all moving to and fro, you just have to know your way around a bit. I know the names of all the important people. You take note of all the costumes and in the evening you tell them in the studio: I am so terribly sleepy; I spent the night at Prince Aldobrandini's ball, or Count Salviati's; the Prince was dressed in such and such a fashion, the Princess in some other—and you are not lying. Come on, take my cape from the back. *(They take their place in the doorway of the house.)*

Goldsmith Did you hear the little idlers? I would like to hear one of my apprentices talk like that!

Merchant All right, all right, Mondella. As long as pleasure costs nothing, youth has nothing to lose. All these little rascals' wide, astounded eyes warm my heart.—That is how I was, sniffing the air and seeking out news. It appears that Nasi's daughter is a strapping wench and Martelli is a lucky young man. Theirs is a good Florentine family! All these great lords have such a fine air! I confess these parties give me a good deal of pleasure. You are in your bed, cozy and peaceful, with an edge of the curtains pulled back; from time to time you look at the lights going back and forth in the palace; you catch a bit of a dance-tune gratis and you say: Ho, ho, that is my cloth dancing, my fine God-given cloth, on the dear bodies of those good, steadfast nobles.

Goldsmith There is more than one that has not been paid for, neighbor. Those are the ones they spill wine on and they scrape against the walls with the least regret. It is quite normal for the great nobles to amuse themselves—they were born for that. But there are amusements of various kinds, if you know what I mean.

Merchant Yes, yes, like dancing, riding, tennis, and so many others. What *do* you mean, Mondella?

Goldmith That will do. —I know what I'm talking about. —I mean that the walls of all those palaces have never proven their solidity better. They needed less strength to protect the ancestors from the falling rain than they do to hold the sons up when they have had too much of their wine.

Merchant A glass of wine is always a good counselor, Mondella. Come into my shop, now, and I shall show you a bolt of velvet.

Goldsmith Yes, always a good counselor and always welcome, neighbor. A good glass of old wine looks very nice at the tip of the arm that sweated to earn it. The honest man who works for his family raises it gaily, with a little flourish, and it goes and warms his heart. But all these court dandies are just shameless hogsheads. Who can you please when you drink yourself into stupor like a wild brute? No one, not even yourself, and God still less.

Merchant Carnival has been pretty rough, I must confess. Their damned balloon ruined fifty florins' worth of my goods. Thank God, the Strozzi paid for it!

Goldsmith The Strozzi! Heaven punish those who dared lay a hand on their nephew! The finest man in Florence is Filippo Strozzi!

Merchant All the same, it was Piero Strozzi who dragged his damned balloon by my shop and made three big stains on a yard of embroidered velvet. By the way, Mondella, shall we be seeing each other at Monteoliveto?

Goldsmith It is not my trade to go to fairs. But I shall go to Monteoliveto out of piety. It is a holy pilgrimage, neighbor, and it atones for every sin.

Merchant And it is quite a venerable one, neighbor, and makes more money for us merchants than any other day of the year. It is a pleasure to see the good ladies as they come out from Mass, handling and looking over all the cloth. God save his Highness! The court is a fine thing.

Goldsmith The court! The people are carrying it on their backs, you know! Florence used to be—and not all that long ago—a good, well-built house. All these great palaces, which are the great families' lodgings, were its columns. There wasn't one among all those columns that stood an inch higher than the rest. They all bore up among themselves an old, well-cemented arch, and we could walk around beneath it without fear of a stone falling on our heads. But there are two ill-advised architects out in the world who have spoiled the whole business, between you and me: the Pope and Emperor Charles.[16] The Emperor started it by entering through a good-sized breach in the aforesaid house. After that, they judged it best to take one of the columns I'm talking about, to wit the Medici family's, and to make it into a steeple, which grew like a damned mushroom in the space of a single night. And then, neighbor, do you know, since the building tottered in the wind, because it was top-heavy and missing one leg, they replaced the pillar that had become a steeple with a big shapeless blob made out of mud and spittle and they called it the citadel. The Germans settled into that damned hole like rats in a wheel of cheese; it is a good thing to know that they are keeping an eye on us even as they play dice and drink their vinegary wine. It doesn't matter how the Florentine families howl and the people and the merchants can say what they want, but the Medici rule by means of their garrison. They devour us, as a poisonous growth devours a sick stomach. It is thanks to the pikes walking back and forth on the bulwark that a bastard, half a Medici, a brute that Heaven meant to be a butcher-boy or a plow-hand, lies in our daughters' beds, drinks our wine, breaks our windows—and we even pay him to do it.

Merchant My goodness! How you do talk! You seem to know all that by heart. It wouldn't be a good idea to say that into just any ears, neighbor Mondella.

Goldsmith And what if they do banish me, like so many others! A man can live just as well in Rome as here. The devil take their wedding festivity, the dancers, and the givers! *(Exit. The merchant mingles with the onlookers. A burgher passes by with his wife.)*

Wife Guglielmo Martelli is a handsome, rich man. What a fine son-in-law he makes for Niccolò Nasi. Look! The ball is still going on.— Ahh, look at all those lights.

Burgher And when are we going to marry off *our* daughter?

Wife How everything is lit up! What a fine party, to be still dancing at this hour.—I heard the Duke is there.

Burgher Turning day into night and night into day is a good way not to see honest folk. A fine business, indeed, to set pikes at the door of a wedding party! God protect our city—every day there are more and more of those German sons-of-bitches coming out of their damned fortress.

Wife Just look at that nice mask. Oh, what a beautiful dress! Oh, dear, all of that costs a lot of money and we are so poor, at home. *(Exeunt.)*

Soldier *(to the merchant)* Look out, rabble, let the horses pass.

Merchant Rabble yourself, you German devil! *(The soldier strikes him with his pike.—the merchant moves away.)* That is how they carry out the terms of the surrender! Those scoundrels mistreat the citizens. *(He goes back into his shop.)*

First Sch. *(to his friend)* Do you see that one over there, taking off his mask? It's Palla Rucellai. He is quite a fellow! The short one, next to him, is Tommaso Strozzi; they call him Masaccio.

Page *(crying)* His Highness's horse!

Second Sch. Let's go, the Duke is coming out of the palace.

First Sch. Do you think he is going to eat you? *(The crowd at the door grows larger.)* That one there is Niccolini. The other one is the Governor. *(Enter the Duke, dressed as a nun, with Giuliano Salviati dressed the same way. Both are wearing masks.)*

Duke *(getting on his horse)* Are you coming, Giuliano?

Salviati No, your Highness, not yet. *(He whispers in his ear.)*

Duke All right, all right, go ahead!

Salviati She is as beautiful as a devil.—Let me go ahead, if I can get rid of my wife. *(He returns to the ball.)*

Duke You are drunk, Salviati. The devil take me, you aren't walking straight. *(He rides off with his retinue.)*

First sch. Now that the Duke has left, it won't go on for long. *(The maskers exit on all sides.)*

Second sch. Pink, green, blue... My eyes are popping and my head is spinning.

Burgher The supper seems to have gone on for quite a while. Look at those two who can't stand up. *(The Governor gets on his horse and a broken bottle falls on his shoulder.)*

Gov. Ha! 'Sblood! What fool let that drop?

Masker Ha, don't you see him, my lord Corsini? Here, look at the window. It is Lorenzo in his nun's habit.

Gov. Lorenzaccio, the devil take you, you have wounded my horse. *(The window shuts.)* The plague take that drunkard and his silent tricks! He is a rascal who has not smiled three times in all his life and who spends his time playing tricks like a schoolboy on holiday. *(Exit. Luisa Strozzi comes out of the house accompanied by Giuliano Salviati. He holds her stirrup for her. She gets on her horse, a squire and a governess follow her.)*

Giuliano A very pretty leg, my dear girl! You are a ray of sunshine and you have burned the very marrow of my bones.

Luisa My lord, that is not fit language for a nobleman.

Giuliano What eyes you have, my dearest heart! What a beautiful shoulder to wipe off, so damp and so cool! What would I have to give you to be your chambermaid tonight? What a pretty foot to undress!

Luisa Let go of my foot, Salviati.

Giuliano No, *corpo di Bacco*, not until you have told me when we shall sleep together. *(Luisa whips her horse and goes off at a gallop.)*

Masker *(to Giuliano)* That little Strozzi girl left as red as a beet. You have angered her, Salviati.

Giuliano Bah! a maiden's anger and the morning rain... *(Exit.)*

Scene 3.

At Marquis de Cibo's house.

(The Marquis is wearing his traveling clothes. The Marquise, their son Ascanio; Cardinal Cibo seated.)

Marquis *(embracing his son)* I wish I could take you with me, little one, you and that great sword you have dragging between your legs. Be patient, Massa is not far and I shall bring you back a fine present.

Marquise Farewell, Lorenzo! Come back soon!

Cardinal Marquise, these tears of yours are really misplaced. You would think my brother was leaving for the Holy Land. I really don't think he is running any great danger on his lands.

Marquis Brother, don't speak ill of those beautiful tears. *(He embraces his wife.)*

Cardinal I just wish that virtue did not look like that.

Marquise Does virtue have no tears, then, Cardinal? Are they only for repentance or for fear?

Marquis No, by heaven, indeed the best ones are for love! Do not wipe these from my face, the wind will take care of that along the way. Let them dry slowly! Well, my dear, don't you have any message for me to give to your favorites? Shall I not bear with me, as usual, some fine sentimental address to make on your behalf to the rocks and waterfalls of my family estate?

Marquise Oh, my poor little cascades!

Marquis It is true, my dearest; they are quite sad without you. *(Lower.)* They used to be so joyful, Ricciarda, weren't they?

Marquise Take me with you!

Marquis I would if I were mad, and I almost am, despite my old soldier's air. Let's speak no more of it.—It will only be a week. I want my dear Ricciarda to see her gardens when they are peaceful and deserted; my farmers' muddy feet will leave no tracks along her cherished pathways. I have to count my old tree-trunks, which remind me of your father, Alberico, and all the blades of grass in my woods. The tenant farmers and their oxen are all my business. At the first flower I see open, I shall put them all out and then I shall take you there.

Marquise The first flower on our beautiful lawn is always dear to me. The winter lasts so long! I always have the feeling that the poor little things will never come back again!

Ascanio Which horse are you riding there, father?

Marquis Come down into the courtyard with me, you will see. *(Exit. The Marquise remains alone with the Cardinal.—A moment of silence.)*

Cardinal Wasn't it today that you asked me to hear your confession, Marquise?

Marquise Please excuse me, Cardinal. We can do it this evening, if Your Eminence is free, or tomorrow, as you wish.—This moment does not belong to me. *(She goes to the window and waves farewell to her husband.)*

Cardinal If regrets were permitted a faithful servant of God, I should envy my brother's fate.—Such a brief trip, so simple, so peaceful!—A visit to one of his estates, only a short way from here!—A week's absence,—and such sadness, I mean such sweet sadness, at his departure! A man who can inspire love like that after seven years of marriage is fortunate! It is seven years, isn't it, Marquise?

Marquise Yes, Cardinal, my son is six years old.

Cardinal Were you at the Nasi's wedding yesterday?

Marquise Yes, I was.

Cardinal And the Duke, dressed as a nun!

Marquise What do you mean, the Duke dressed as a nun?

Cardinal I had been told that he wore that costume. I may have been misled.

Marquise Indeed, he was. Oh, Malaspina, we are living in a sad time for all sacred matters!

Cardinal One may respect sacred matters and still, on a day of exuberance, put on the habit of certain convents without any hostile intent toward the holy Catholic church.

Marquise The example is to be feared, not the intent. I am not like you; it offended me deeply. It is true that I do not really know what can and cannot be done, according to your mysterious rules. God knows what they will lead to. Those who put words on their anvils and twist them with a hammer and a file do not always reflect that those words represent thoughts, and those thoughts actions.

Cardinal Well, well, the Duke is young, Marquise, and I'll wager his charming nun's habit looked adorable on him.

Marquise Absolutely perfect. All it lacked were a few drops of the blood of his cousin, Ippolito de' Medici.[17]

Cardinal And a Phrygian cap, my little sister, am I not right? What hatred for the poor Duke!

Marquise And it is all the same to you, his right arm, for the Duke to be Emperor Charles's deputy, the Pope's civil agent, as Baccio is his religious agent? It is all the same to you, brother of my Lorenzo, for our sun to cast German shadows on the citadel? For the Emperor to speak through everyone's mouth here? For depravity to act as a pimp for slavery and jingle its bells over the people's sobs? Oh, the clergy would ring all their bells, if need be, to muffle its sound and to reawaken the imperial eagle, if it were to fall asleep on our poor roofs. *(Exit.)*

Cardinal *(alone, raising the tapestry and calling softly)* Agnolo! *(Enter a page.)* What is new today?

Agnolo This letter, monsignor.

Cardinal Give it to me.

Agnolo Alas, Eminence, that is a sin.

Cardinal Nothing is a sin when you are obeying a priest of the Church of Rome. *(Agnolo gives him the letter.)* It is comical to hear the ravings of that poor Marquise and to see her running, bathed in republican tears, to a tryst with our beloved tyrant. *(He opens the letter and reads it.)*

> "Either you will belong to me or you will certainly bring about my downfall, yours, and that of our two houses."

The Duke writes tersely, but his style does not lack a certain vigor. What is hard to know is whether the Marquise was persuaded or not. Two months of assiduous wooing is a lot for Alessandro. It ought to be sufficient for Ricciarda Cibo. *(He gives the letter back to the page.)* Put that back in your mistress's room. You will remain silent, of course. You may count on me. *(He gives him his hand to kiss and exits.)*

Scene 4.

A courtyard in the Duke's palace.

(Duke Alessandro on a terrace; some pages are exercising horses in the courtyard. Enter Valori and Lord Maurizio.)

Duke *(to Valori)* Has Your Eminence received news from the court at Rome this morning?

Valori Paul III[18] sends a thousand blessings to Your Highness, and expresses his most ardent good wishes for your prosperity.

Duke Nothing but good wishes, Valori?

Valori His Holiness fears that the Duke is creating new dangers by excessive indulgence. The people are ill accustomed to absolute power. The Emperor said as much to Your Highness during his latest voyage, I believe.

Duke By God, What a fine horse, Lord Maurizio! Ha, that is the devil's own rump![19]

Maurizio Magnificent, Your Highness.

Duke So, my esteemed apostolic deputy, there are still a few dead branches to prune. The Emperor and the Pope have made me king,[20] but, by God! they put a kind of scepter in my hand that smells of the executioner's ax for miles around. Come now, Valori, what do you want?

Valori I am a clergyman, Your Highness. If the words that my duty obliges me to report faithfully to you must be interpreted in such a grim manner, my heart forbids me to add a single word.

Duke Yes, yes, I know you are a good man. By God, you are the only honest priest I have seen in all my life.

Valori My lord, honesty is neither lost nor gained under any habit, and there are more good men than bad ones.

Duke And so, no explanations?

Maurizio May I speak, my Lord? It is all quite easy to explain.

Duke Well, then?

Maurizio The court's excesses trouble the Pope.

Duke What is that you are saying?

Maurizio I said the *court's* excesses, Your Highness. The Duke's actions have no other judge than himself. It is Lorenzo de' Medici[21] that the Pope claims as a fugitive from his justice.

Duke From his justice? He never offended any Pope, as far as I know, except Clement VII, my late cousin who, at this moment, is down in hell.

Maurizio Clement VII let escape from his territories the libertine who, one day when he was drunk, had decapitated the statues on the Arch of Constantine.[22] Paul III could never pardon the official model of Florentine vice.

Duke Ha, by God, Alessandro Farnese[23] is a droll fellow! If vice bothers him so, what the devil is he going to do about his bastard son, our dear Pietro Farnese, who has treated the Bishop of Fano so pleasantly?[24] That mutilation keeps coming up in connection with poor Renzo. I, for one, find it funny to have cut off the heads of all those men of stone. I foster the arts like the next man and I have some of the best artists in Italy at my court. But I just cannot understand the Pope's respect for those statues, which he would excommunicate tomorrow if they were flesh and blood.

Maurizio Lorenzo is an atheist. He ridicules everything. If Your Highness's government is not surrounded with the profoundest respect, it cannot be stable. The people call Lorenzo "Lorenzaccio." It is known that he is charged with your pleasures and that is enough.

Duke Silence! You are forgetting that Lorenzo de' Medici is Alessandro's cousin. *(Enter Cardinal Cibo.)* Cardinal, just listen to these gentlemen, who are saying that the Pope is scandalized by the excesses of poor Renzo and who claim it is harming my authority.

Cardinal Messer Francesco Molza has just pronounced a disquisition in Latin in the Roman academy against the man who mutilated the Arch of Constantine.

Duke Come now, you could get me angry! Renzo, someone to be feared—the most arrant coward! That effeminate weakling, that shadow of a spiritless pander! That dreamer, who goes without a sword night and day for fear of seeing its shadow beside him! Besides, he is a philosopher, a paper scratcher, a wretched poet who can't even write a sonnet! No, no, I am not frightened yet by shadows. Ha! Corpo di Bacco! What do Latin disquisitions and my rabble's gossip matter to me! I love Lorenzo, God damn it, and here he shall remain.

Cardinal If I feared the man, it would not be for your court or for Florence. It would be for yourself, Duke.

Duke Are you joking, Cardinal? Do you want me to tell you the truth? *(He speaks softly to him.)* Everything I know about those damned exiles, about all those stubborn republicans plotting against me, I know through Lorenzo. He is slippery as an eel. He worms his way into everything and he tells me all. He has even found a way to carry on a correspondence with all those God-damned Strozzis! Yes, of course, he is my procurer; but you may take it from me, his procuring does not hurt me if it hurts anyone. Look! *(Lorenzo appears at the end of a low passageway.)* Just look at that skinny little body, that walking hangover. Look at those glassy eyes, those weak, sickly hands, hardly strong enough to hold up a lady's fan; that gloomy face, which sometimes smiles but hasn't the force to laugh. Is that a man to be feared? Come, come, you must be joking. Hey,

Renzo, come on over here. Lord Maurizio here is looking to have an argument with you.

Lorenzo *(coming up the stairs to the terrace)* May I wish you good morning, my cousin's friends?

Duke Lorenzo, listen to this. We have been talking about you for an hour now. Have you heard the news? My friend, you have been excommunicated in Latin and Lord Maurizio says you are a dangerous man. So does the Cardinal. As for my good friend Valori, he is too polite to pronounce your name.

Lorenzo Dangerous for whom, Your Eminence? For bawds or for the saints in Paradise?

Cardinal The dogs in court can catch rabies, just like other dogs.

Lorenzo A priest's insult ought to be said in Latin.

Maurizio There are some in plain language that a man might answer.

Lorenzo Ah, Lord Maurizio, I hadn't seen you. Forgive me, the sun was in my eyes. But you are looking well and I believe your clothes are brand new.[25]

Maurizio Like your wit. I had them made out of one of my grandfather's old doublets.

Lorenzo Cousin, when you are tired of some village conquest, please send her over to Lord Maurizio. It is unwholesome to be living without a woman, for a man like him who has a short neck and furry hands.

Maurizio A man who thinks he has the right to joke ought to know how to defend himself. If I were you, I would get a sword.

Lorenzo If anyone has told you I am a soldier, it is a mistake. I am a poor seeker of knowledge.

Maurizio Your wit is a sharp but flexible sword. It is too base a weapon. Each man uses what he has. *(He draws his sword.)*

Valori A drawn sword, in the Duke's presence!

Duke *(laughing)* Let them be, let them be. Come now, Renzo, I shall be your second. Someone give him a sword.

Lorenzo My lord, what are you saying?

Duke Well, well, has your flippancy evaporated so quickly? Are you trembling, cousin? Fie on you! You are a disgrace to the name of Medici. I am only a bastard: can I wear it better than you who are legitimate? A sword, a sword, a Medici does not let himself be challenged like that. Pages, come on up here. The whole court will see it and I wish all Florence were here.

Lorenzo Your Highness is joking.

Duke I was joking a little while ago but now I am blushing with shame. A sword! *(He takes a sword from a page and presents it to Lorenzo.)*

Valori My lord, this is carrying things too far. A sword drawn in Your Highness's presence is a punishable crime inside the palace.

Duke Who speaks here when I am speaking?

Valori Your Highness cannot have had any other aim that to have a moment's fun and Lord Maurizio himself acted with no other thought in mind.

Duke And don't you see that I am still joking! Who the devil is thinking of a serious affair here? Just look at Renzo: his knees are shaking. He would have grown pale, if he could. What a face, good God, I think he is going to fall down! *(Lorenzo staggers; he leans on the balustrade and suddenly slips to the ground.)*

Duke *(laughing uproariously)* What did I tell you? No one knows it better than I do: the mere sight of a sword makes him dizzy. Come now, my dear Lorenzetta, have them carry you back to your mother's house. *(The pages pick up Lorenzo.)*

Maurizio You double coward! You son of a whore!

Duke Be silent, Lord Maurizio. Watch your words. It is I who am telling you now: no talk like that in my presence.[26] *(Exit Lord Maurizio.)*

Valori The poor young man!

Cardinal *(remaining alone with the Duke)* Do you believe all that, my lord?

Duke I would just like to know why I shouldn't.

Cardinal Hmm! It is a bit much.

Duke That is precisely why I believe it. Can you imagine that a Medici would shame himself in public, just for pleasure? In any case, that is not the first time it has happened to him. He has never been able to bear the sight of a sword.

Cardinal It is a bit much. It is a bit much. *(Exeunt.)*

Scene 5.

Before the church of San Miniato in Monteoliveto.[27]

(A crowd is coming out of the church.)

Woman *(to her neighbor)* Are you returning to Florence this evening?

Neighbor I don't ever stay here more than an hour and I never come more than just one Friday. I am not rich enough to stop at the fair. For me it is simply a religious matter. If it is enough for my salvation, that is all I need.

A Court Lady How well he preached! He is my daughter's confessor. *(She walks toward a shop.)* White and gold is very nice in the evening; but by daylight there is no way to keep it looking clean.

The merchant and the goldsmith are standing in front of their shops with some noblemen.)

Goldsmith The citadel! The people will never accept it: to see this new Tower of Babel suddenly rise up over the city, amid the damnedest jabbering! The Germans will never take root in Florence and to graft them here will take a very strong bond.

Merchant Look here, ladies. Won't your ladyships take a stool here under my awning?

Nobleman You come from old Florentine stock, Mondella. Hatred of tyranny still makes your wrinkled hands shake as you execute your prized carvings in the back of your shop.

Goldsmith That is true, your Excellency. If I were a great artist I would love princes, because only they can undertake great projects. Great artists have no motherland. As for me, I carve holy vessels and sword handles.

Another Noble. Speaking of artists, do you see the big fellow over there in that little tavern, who is gesticulating in front of a crowd? He is rapping his glass on the table. Unless I am wrong, it is that braggart, Cellini.[28]

First Noble. Let's go over and enter, then. With a glass of wine under his belt, he is worth hearing. He is probably telling some interesting tale. *(Exeunt. Two burghers sit down.)*

First Burgher Has there been a riot in Florence?

Second Burgher Practically nothing. A few poor young fellows were killed in the Old Market.

First Burgher What a pity for their families!

Second Burgher That sort of misfortune is inevitable. What can you expect young people to do under a government like ours?[29] Someone comes along and announces with a fanfare of trumpets that the Emperor is in Bologna; so the idlers repeat, "The Emperor is in Bologna," with winks and knowing looks, not reflecting on what he might be doing there. The next day, they are still happier to learn and repeat, "The Pope is in Bologna with the Emperor."[30] What comes next? Public rejoicing, that is all they see in it. And then one fine morning they wake up with their heads all in a fog from the Emperor's wine, and they see a sinister face in the great window of the Pazzi palace. They ask who that individual is and the answer is that he is their king. The Pope and the Emperor have given birth to a bastard who has the power of life and death over our children and who couldn't name his own mother.

Goldsmith (coming over) Spoken like a patriot, my friend. I would advise you to watch out for that great lout over there. *(A German officer passes by.)*

Officer Move off, gentlemen. There are some ladies who want to sit down. *(Two ladies of the court enter and sit down.)*

First Lady Is this from Venice?

Merchant Yes, your Ladyship, it is splendid. Shall I cut off a few yards of it for you?

First Lady If you would. I thought I saw Giuliano Salviati pass by.

Officer He is walking back and forth in front of the church door. What a philanderer!

Second Lady What a cad! Show me some silk stockings.

Officer There won't be any small enough for you.

First Lady Oh, stop, you don't know what to say. Since you have seen Giuliano, go tell him that I have to speak to him.

Officer All right, I shall bring him right back. *(Exit.)*

First Lady Your officer is as stupid as anyone could wish. Whatever can you be doing with something of that kind?

Second Lady Let me tell you, there is nothing better than a man like him. *(They go off. Enter the Prior of Capua.)*[31]

Prior Give me a glass of lemonade, my good man. *(He sits down.)*

First Burgher That is the Prior of Capua. He is a real patriot! *(The two burghers sit down again.)*

Prior Have you been to church, gentlemen? What did you think of the sermon?

First Burgher It was a fine one, your Reverence.

Second Burgher *(to the goldsmith)* The Strozzi's nobility is dear to the common people because they are not proud. Isn't it gratifying to see a great lord speaking freely with his fellows, in a friendly manner? That is a good deal more important than you might think.

Prior If I must speak frankly, I found the sermon a bit too fine. I have preached in my time and I never took great pride in shaking the windows. But a little tear rolling down the cheek of a good man always seemed quite precious to me. *(Enter Salviati.)*

Salviati I was told that there were some women asking for me a moment ago. But I don't see any robes here except yours, Prior. Was I mistaken?

Merchant Your Excellency, you weren't mistaken. The ladies have gone off but I think they will be back. There are ten yards of fabric and four pairs of stockings here for them.

Salviati *(sitting down)* That is such a pretty woman, going by.—Now where the devil have I seen her?—Oh, of course, it was in my bed!

Prior *(to the burgher)* I think I have seen your signature on a letter addressed to the Duke.

First Burgher I admit it openly: it was on the petition from the exiles.

Prior Do you have any in your family?

First Burgher Two, your Excellency: my father and my uncle. I am the only man left in our house.

Second Burgher (to the goldsmith) What a nasty tongue that Salviati has!

Goldsmith That is not surprising: a man who is half bankrupt, living off the Medici's generosity, and married as he is to a woman who has lost whatever honor she possessed! He would like what they say of his wife to be said of all women.

Salviati Isn't that Luisa Strozzi going by on that knoll?

Merchant Indeed, your lordship. There are few of our noble ladies that I do not know. If I am not mistaken, that is her younger sister holding her hand.

Salviati I met that Luisa last night at the Nasi's ball. My word, she has very pretty legs. We are to sleep together at the earliest opportunity.

Prior *(turning around)* What do you mean?

Salviati It is quite clear. She told me so. I was holding the stirrup for her, quite innocently. Somehow or other I grasped her leg and that is how it all came about.

Prior Giuliano, I do not know whether you are aware that you are speaking of my sister.

Salviati I am quite aware of it. All women are meant to sleep with men and your sister can very well sleep with me.

Prior *(rising)* Do I owe you anything, my good man? *(He tosses a coin on the table and exits.)*

Salviati I really like that good Prior, who forgets his change because of something said about his sister. You would think that all the virtue in Florence had taken refuge at the Strozzi's. Just look at him turning around. You can stare at me all you want, you won't frighten me. *(Exit.)*

Scene 6.

The banks of the Arno.

(Maria Soderini, Caterina Ginori.)

Caterina The sun is beginning to set. Broad purple streaks pierce through the foliage and beneath the reeds the frogs are ringing their little crystal bells. How strange these evening harmonies seem against the distant noise of our city.

Maria It is time to go home. Tie your scarf around your neck.

Caterina Not yet, unless you are getting cold. Look, my dearest mother. See how beautiful the sky is! How vast and calm it all is! God is everywhere! But you bend your head; you have been looking worried since this morning.

Maria Not worried, but grieved. Didn't you hear them repeating that terrible story about Lorenzo. Now he is the talk of Florence.

Caterina Oh, mother, cowardice is no crime. Courage is not a virtue: why should weakness be subject to blame? It is a sorry privilege to be able to answer for the beating of one's heart. God alone can make it noble and worthy of admiration. Why should that child not have the right that all of us women have? A woman who is afraid of nothing is not likable, or so they say.

Maria Would you love a man who is afraid? You are blushing, Caterina; Lorenzo is your nephew, so you cannot love him. But just imagine if he had a completely different name, what would you think then? What woman would want to lean on his arm to mount on horseback? What man would shake his hand?

Caterina That is sad and yet it is not what I pity him for. Perhaps his heart is not that of a Medici; but alas, it is even less that of a decent man.

Maria Let's not talk of that, Caterina—it is very cruel for a mother not to be able to speak of her son.

Caterina Oh, Florence! That was his undoing! Have I not seen the flame of a noble ambition shining in his eyes at times? Was not his youth the dawn of a rising sun? I often think I still can see a glint today...— I think in spite of myself that everything is not yet dead in him.

Maria Oh, all that is so unfathomable! Such ability, such a sweet love of solitude! My Renzo will never be a warrior, I told myself when I saw him coming home from school bathed in sweat with his arms laden with heavy books; but a holy love of truth shone on his lips and in his dark eyes. He had to worry about everything, say constantly: "That man is poor, that one is ruined. What can be done?" And his admiration for the great men in his Plutarch! Caterina, Caterina, how often, as I kissed his brow, I thought of the father of our country!

Caterina Don't torture yourself.

Maria I say that I do not want to talk about him but I talk about him constantly. You see, there are certain things that mothers stop talking of only in the silence of eternity. If my son had been an ordinary debauchee, if the Soderini's blood had run pale in that little drop fallen from my veins, I would not be in despair. But I had hopes and for good reason. Oh, Caterina, he is no longer even handsome. Like some evil smoke, the stain in his heart has risen up onto his face. His smile, that sweet bloom that makes youth seem so like flowers, has fled his sulfur-yellow cheeks and left ignoble irony and universal disdain to grumble there instead.

Caterina He is still handsome at times in his strange melancholy.

Maria Did not his birth call him to the throne? Could he not have brought to it the knowledge of a scholar, the brightest youth in the world, and crowned all my most cherished dreams with a golden diadem? Should I not have expected that? Oh, Kate, if you wish to sleep in peace, it is better not to have had certain dreams. It is too cruel to have lived in a fairy castle where angels sang sweet hymns, to have fallen asleep in it, cradled by your son, and to wake up in a bloody hovel filled with the debris of orgies and human remains, in the arms of a horrid ghost that kills while still calling you by the name of mother.

Caterina Silent shadows are beginning to walk along the road. Let us go back home, Maria, all these exiles frighten me.

Maria The poor men! We ought to feel nothing but pity for them! Oh, can't I see a single thing without a thorn piercing my heart? Can I no longer open my eyes? Alas, Kate, all this is more of Lorenzo's work. All those poor citizens trusted him. There is not one among all those fathers banished from their land who was not betrayed by my son. Their letters, signed with their names, are shown to the Duke. In that way he even twists the glorious memory of his ancestors into an ignoble use. Lovers of the republic turn to him as to the ancient progeny of their protector. His household is open to them, even the Strozzi themselves come there. Poor Filippo! Your gray hair will come to a sad end! Oh, can I not see a shameless girl, an unfortunate wretch deprived of his family, without all that crying out to me: You are the mother of our misfortunes! When shall I be here? *(She strikes the earth.)*

Caterina My poor mother, your tears are contagious. *(They go off.—The sun has set.—A group of exiles forms in the middle of a field.)*

An exile Where are you headed?

Another To Pisa. What about you?

First exile To Rome.

Another And I am off to Venice. Those two are going to Ferrara. What will become of us, so far away from each other?

A fourth Farewell, neighbor, till better times. *(He goes off.)*

Second Farewell. As for us, we can walk together until the cross of the Virgin. *(He leaves with another one.—Enter Maffio.)*

First exile Is that you, Maffio? What brings you here?

Maffio I am one of you. You must know that the Duke abducted my sister. I drew my sword and some sort of tiger, with arms of steel, grabbed hold of me and disarmed me. After which I was given the order to leave the city along with a purse half-full of ducats.

Second And where is your sister?

Maffio They showed her to me this evening, coming out of the theater wearing a dress even the Empress doesn't own. God forgive her! An old woman was with her; she left three of her teeth at the door. Never in my life have I thrown a punch that gave me such pleasure.

Third May they all die like dogs in their foul muck and then we can die happy.

Fourth Filippo Strozzi will write to us in Venice. One of these days we shall all be astonished to find an army at our command.

Third Long live Filippo! As long as he has one hair on his head, liberty will not be dead in Italy. *(One part of the group goes off; all the exiles embrace each other.)*

A voice Until better times.

Another Till better times. *(Two exiles go up onto a platform from which the city can be seen.)*

First Farewell, Florence, plague of Italy. Farewell, barren mother who has no more milk for your children.

Second Farewell, bastard Florence, horrid specter of the ancient Florence. Farewell, unspeakable muck.

All the exiles Farewell, Florence! A curse on your women's breasts! A curse on your tears! A curse on the prayers in your churches, on the bread of your wheat, on the air in your streets! Cursed be the last drop of your corrupt blood!

ACT TWO

Scene 1.

The Strozzi palace.

Filippo *(in his study)* Ten citizens exiled from just this neighborhood! Old Galeazzo and young Maffio in exile! His sister shamed, turned into a harlot in just one night! The poor girl! When will the education of the lower classes be strong enough to keep young girls from laughing while their parents weep? Is corruption really a law of nature? Is what we call virtue just Sunday dress that we put on to go to church? The rest of the week they sit knitting at the window and watching the young men go by. Poor humankind! Which name do you bear, then, that of your race or that of your baptism? And what original stain have we poor old dreamers washed from the face of humanity in the four or five thousand years that we have been turning yellow along with our books? How easy it is for you, in the silence of your study, to trace a line as pure and fine as a hair with a light hand on this white paper! How easy it is for you to build palaces and cities with this pair of compasses and a little ink! But the architect who has thousands of admirable plans in his desk cannot raise the first stone of his edifice off the ground, when he goes and sets to work with his stooped back and his stubborn ideas. For men's happiness to be merely a dream is terribly hard to bear. For evil to be irrevocable, eternal, impossible to alter—no! Why should the philosopher working for the common good look about him? That is wrong. The tiniest insect passing before his eyes hides the sun from him. So let us go forth more boldly. A republic—that is the word we must have. And even if it should merely be a word, that is something, since nations arise when it rings out through the air... Ah, hello, Leone. *(Enter the Prior of Capua.)*

Prior I have just come from the fair at Monteoliveto.

Filippo Was it fine? So here you are, too, Piero. Come and sit down, I have to speak with you. *(Enter Piero Strozzi.)*

Prior It was very fine and I had a very good time there, apart from a certain vexation that I find a bit too hard to digest.

Piero Bah! What was it?

Prior Just imagine, I went into a shop to have a glass of lemonade... —No, it is useless, I am a fool even to recall it.

Filippo What the devil is troubling you? You are talking like a soul in Hell.

Prior It is nothing. Just some nasty things said, nothing more. No significance should be attached to any of that.

Piero Things said? About whom? About you?

Prior Not exactly about me. What do I care for things said about me?

Piero About whom, then? Come on, speak up if you want to.

Prior It is wrong of me. One should not remember things like that when one knows the difference between a decent man and a Salviati.

Piero Salviati? What did that scoundrel say?

Prior He is a wretch, you are right. What does it matter what he can say? A man with no shame, a court lackey who, from what people say, has a licentious jade for a wife! Come, now, that is all, I shall not think of it any more.

Piero Think of it and speak, Leone. I mean, I am just itching to cut his ears off. Whom did he speak ill of? Of us? Of my father? Oh, Christ's blood, I do not much like that Salviati. I have to know, do you understand?

Prior If you insist, I shall tell you. He expressed himself in my presence, in a shop, in a truly offensive way, about our sister.

Piero Oh, my God! In what terms? Come on now, speak up!

Prior In the grossest terms.

Piero You damned priest! You see that I am beside myself with impatience and you pick and choose your words! Say things as they are. Damn it, a word is a word, God or no God.

Filippo Piero, Piero, you are being disrespectful to your brother.

Prior He said he would sleep with her, that is the word he used, and that she had promised him to.

Piero She would sleep... Oh, Christ Jesus! What time is it?

Filippo Where are you going? Come now, are you made of gunpowder? What do you think you are going to do with that sword? You already have one at your side.

Piero I have nothing to do. Let us go have dinner, dinner is served. *(Exeunt.)*

Scene 2.

The doorway of a church.

(Enter Lorenzo and Valori.)

Valori How is it the Duke has not yet come? Oh, my good sir, what a great satisfaction these magnificent ceremonies of the Roman church are for a Christian! What sort of man can resist them? Does the artist not find in them the paradise of his heart? Do not the warrior, the priest, and the merchant encounter all that they love in them? The captivating harmony of the organ, the lustrous velvet hangings and tapestries, the paintings by first-rate masters, the sweet and subtle perfumes rising from the censers, and the delightful singing of the silvery voices—all that may shock the austere monk and the enemy of pleasure by its sensuousness. But for me nothing is more beautiful than a religion that appeals through such means. Why should priests wish to serve a jealous God? Religion is not a bird of prey, it is a compassionate dove, soaring gently over all dreams and all loves.

Lorenzo Of course. What you are saying is perfectly true and perfectly false, like everything else in the world.

Tebaldeo *(coming up to Valori)* Oh, Monsignor, how sweet it is to hear a man such as Your Eminence speak thus of tolerance and holy fervor! Please excuse an obscure citizen who burns with divine ardor[32] if he thanks you for those few words I have just heard. It is the greatest pleasure one can desire, to find what one feels in one's heart on the lips of a good man.

Valori Aren't you young Freccia?

Tebaldeo My works have little value. I know the love of art better than how to practice it. My entire youth has been spent in churches.

I feel as if I could not admire Raphael and our divine Michelangelo[33] anywhere else. And so I remain for days on end, contemplating their works in absolute ecstasy. The music of the organ reveals their thoughts and helps me penetrate their souls. I look at the figures in their paintings, kneeling so piously, and I listen as though the hymns of the choir were issuing forth from their parted lips. Clouds of aromatic incense pass between them and me in a light haze. I imagine I see the glory of the artist in them; but it is also a sad, sweet mist, which would be but a sterile perfume if it did not rise up to God.

Valori You have the heart of a true artist. Come to my palace and bring something under your cloak when you do. I want you to work for me.

Tebaldeo Your Eminence does me too great an honor. I am a very humble servant of the holy religion of painting.

Lorenzo Why put off your offers of service? It looks to me as if you have a canvas there in your hands.

Tebaldeo That is true. But I do not dare show it to such great connoisseurs. It is the poor sketch of a magnificent dream.

Lorenzo So you do portraits of your dreams? I shall have some of mine pose for you.

Tebaldeo Materializing dreams is the very life of painters. The greatest ones have represented theirs in all their force without changing a thing. Their imagination was a tree whose sap ran freely; its buds blossomed forth effortlessly into flowers, and its flowers into fruit. Soon those fruits matured under invigorating sunlight, and when they were ripe they came loose by themselves and fell to the ground without losing a single grain of their virginal pollen. Alas, the dreams of mediocre artists are difficult plants to foster: they are watered with bitter tears and only reach a lowly fruition. *(He shows them his picture.)*

Valori In all honesty, that is quite fine. Not of the very first rank it is true—why should I flatter a man who does not flatter himself? But your face is still beardless, young man.

Lorenzo Is it a landscape or a portrait? Which way should we look at it, lengthwise or breadth wise?

Tebaldeo Your Lordship is mocking me. It is a view of the Camposanto cemetery.

Lorenzo How far is it from here to immortality?

Valori It is wrong to make fun of this young man. See how each of your words makes his eyes grow sad.

Tebaldeo Immortality is faith. Those to whom God has given wings get there with a smile on their faces.

Valori You talk like a pupil of Raphael's.

Tebaldeo My lord, he was my teacher. All I know comes from him.

Lorenzo Come to my place. I shall have you paint Mazzafirra in the nude.

Tebaldeo I may not have any respect for my brush but I do for my art. I cannot paint the portrait of a harlot.

Lorenzo Your God did go to the trouble of making her, so at least you could take the trouble to paint her. Would you paint a view of Florence for me?

Tebaldeo Yes, my lord.

Lorenzo How would you go about it?

Tebaldeo I would view her from the East, on the left bank of the Arno. That is where the perspective is broadest and most pleasant.

Lorenzo So you would paint Florence, her squares, her houses, and her streets?

Tebaldeo Yes, my lord.

Lorenzo So why can't you paint a harlot, if you can paint a brothel?

Tebaldeo I have not been taught to speak thus of my mother.

Lorenzo What are you calling your mother?

Tebaldeo Florence, my lord.

Lorenzo Then you are nothing but a bastard, for your mother is nothing but a whore.

Tebaldeo A bleeding wound can cause corruption in the healthiest of bodies. But from the precious drops of my mother's blood there issues forth a fragrant plant that heals every ill. Art, that divine flower, at times needs manure to fertilize the soil that bears it.

Lorenzo What do you mean?

Tebaldeo Peaceable and happy nations have sometimes shone with a pure but feeble light. The angels' harps have many strings; the western breeze can whisper on the weakest ones and draw from their harmony sweet and delightful chords. But a silver string resonates only when the north wind blows. It is the most beautiful and noble and yet the touch of a rough hand arouses it. Enthusiasm is kin to suffering.

Lorenzo In other words, an unhappy people makes for great artists. I shall be happy to make myself an alchemist with your still; the tears of nations trickle like pearls into it. The devil take it, I do like you. Families can grieve, nations die in poverty, it all stimulates the gentleman's brain. What an admirable poet! How do you reconcile all that with your piety?

Tebaldeo I do not laugh at families' misfortunes: I mean that poetry is the sweetest of sorrows and that she loves her sisters. I pity unhappy peoples but I do in faith believe that they make for great artists. Battlefields make crops grow, corrupt soils foster heaven's grain.

Lorenzo Your doublet is worn. Would you like one in my livery?

Tebaldeo I belong to no one. When thought seeks its freedom, the body must as well.

Lorenzo I feel like having my valet beat you with his stick.

Tebaldeo Why, my lord?

Lorenzo Just because it passes through my mind. Have you had that limp from birth or was it an accident?

Tebaldeo I do not have a limp. What do you mean by that?

Lorenzo You are either lame or you are mad.

Tebaldeo Why, my lord? You are making fun of me.

Lorenzo If you were not lame, why would you remain, unless you were mad, in a city where, in honor of your ideas on freedom, any valet of a Medici who comes along can have you beaten up without anyone saying a thing against it.[34]

Tebaldeo I love my Florence; that is why I remain with her. I know that a citizen can be assassinated in broad daylight in the middle of the street, on the whim of those who govern her. That is why I wear this dagger in my belt.

Lorenzo Would you strike the Duke if the Duke struck you, as has often happened, committing prankish murders just for the fun of it?

Tebaldeo I would kill him if he attacked me.

Lorenzo You are telling that to me?

Tebaldeo Who could wish me harm? I do not harm anyone. I spend my days in the studio. On Sundays I go to Sant'Annunziata or Santa Maria. The monks think I have a good voice. They dress me in a white robe and a red skullcap and I sing my part in the chorus, sometimes a little solo. Those are the only times I go out in public. In the evening I go to my mistress's house and when the night is clear I spend it on her balcony. No one knows me and I know no one: to whom could my life or my death be of any use?

Lorenzo Are you for a republic? Do you love princes?

Tebaldeo I am an artist. I love my mother and my mistress.

Lorenzo Come to my palace tomorrow. I want to have you paint an important picture for my wedding-day. *(Exeunt.)*

Scene 3.

Marquise Cibo's apartment.

Cardinal *(alone)* Yes, I shall carry out your orders, Farnese! Let your apostolic representative shut himself up with his integrity within the narrow circle of his office; I will stir with a firm hand the slippery ground on which he dares not walk. You expect that of me. I understand and I shall act without speaking, as you ordered. You realized who I was when you placed me beside Alessandro without conferring on me any title that might give me power over him. He will be mistrustful of others and obey me without knowing it. Let him exhaust his strength against shadows of men swollen with a shadow of power: I shall be the invisible ring that will bind him hand and foot to the iron chain whose two ends Rome and the Emperor hold. If my eyes do not deceive me, the hammer that I shall use is in this house. Alessandro is in love with my sister-in-law. It is not unbelievable that his love should flatter her; what may come of it remains in doubt. But what she wishes to do with it is quite evident to me. Who knows how far a zealous woman's influence might go, even with such a crude man, that living suit of armor? Such a sweet sin for such a fine cause is tempting, is it not, Ricciarda? To press that lion's heart to your own frail heart, pierced through and through with bloody arrows like Saint Sebastian's; to speak of the country's misfortunes with your eyes brimful of tears, while the beloved tyrant passes his rough hands through your loosened hair; to make the holy spark leap forth from a rock: that was well worth the slight sacrifice of conjugal honor and a few other trifles. Florence would gain so much and our good husbands lose nothing thereby! But you ought not to have taken me for your confessor.

Here she comes, with her prayer-book in her hand. So everything is going to be revealed today. Just let your secret fall into the ears of this priest; as a courtier, he might well take advantage of it; but in all good conscience, he won't tell a word. *(Enter Marquise Cibo. The Cardinal sits down.)* I am ready. *(The Marquise kneels by him on her prie-Dieu.)*

Marquise Bless me, father, for I have sinned.

Cardinal Have you said your *Confiteor*? We may begin, Marquise.

Marquise I have had fits of anger, of sacrilegious and offensive doubts concerning our Holy Father the Pope.

Cardinal Go on.

Marquise Yesterday I said in a group of people, concerning the Bishop of Fano, that the Holy Catholic Church was a den of debauchery.

Cardinal Go on.

Marquise I listened to words contrary to the fidelity I have sworn to my husband.

Cardinal Who spoke those words to you?[35]

Marquise I read a letter written in the same intention.

Cardinal Who wrote that letter to you?

Marquise I am confessing what I have done, not what others have done.

Cardinal Daughter, you must answer me if you want me to be able to give you absolution in complete security. Above all, tell me if you answered that letter.

Marquise I answered verbally but not in writing.

Cardinal What did you answer?

Marquise I granted the person who wrote me permission to see me as he requested.

Cardinal How did that conversation go?

Marquise I have already confessed that I listened to words contrary to my honor.

Cardinal How did you answer them?

Marquise As befits a woman who respects herself.

Cardinal Did you not leave any hope at all that you might be persuaded in the end?

Marquise No, father.

Cardinal Did you tell the person in question you were resolved no longer to listen to such words in the future?

Marquise Yes, father.

Cardinal Do you find that person attractive?

Marquise I hope my heart has no such idea.

Cardinal Have you informed your husband?

Marquise No, father. A virtuous woman should not trouble her marriage with tales of this sort.

Cardinal You are hiding nothing from me? Nothing happened between you and the person in question that you hesitate to confide in me?

Marquise Nothing, father.

Cardinal Not a tender glance? Not a stolen kiss?

Marquise No, father.

Cardinal Is that quite sure, daughter?

Marquise Brother-in-law, I do not think I am in the habit of lying to God.

Cardinal You refused to tell me the name I asked you for a while ago. I cannot give you absolution without knowing it, however.

Marquise Why not? It might be a sin to read a letter but not to read its signature. What does the name matter?

Cardinal It is more important than you think.

Marquise Malaspina, you want to know too much. Deny me absolution if you wish, I shall take the first priest who comes along as a confessor and he will give it to me. *(She rises.)*

Cardinal Such violence, Marquise! As if I didn't know it is the Duke you are referring to.

Marquise The Duke!—Well, if you know that, why do you want to make me say it?

Cardinal Why do you refuse to? I am surprised.

Marquise And what do you want to do with it, as my confessor? Is it because you want to repeat it to my husband that you are so anxious to hear it? Yes, that must be it: it is a bad idea to have a family relation as one's confessor. Heaven knows that when I kneel before you I forget that I am your sister-in-law. But you take care to remind me of it. Beware of your eternal damnation, Cibo, even if you are a Cardinal.

Cardinal Come on back here, Marquise. The offense is not so great as you may believe.

Marquise What do you mean?

Cardinal A confessor must know everything because he can guide everything. But a brother-in-law does not have to tell anything, given certain conditions.

Marquise What conditions?

Cardinal No, no, I was wrong. That was not the word I wanted to use. I meant that the Duke is powerful, that a break with him might harm the richest of families. But a secret of importance, in experienced hands, may become an abundant source of benefits.

Marquise A source of benefits!—Experienced hands!—To tell the truth, I am dumbstruck. What are you brewing beneath those ambiguous expressions, priest? There are certain combinations of words that pass through you priests' lips on occasion that one doesn't know quite how to take.

Cardinal Come back and sit down here, Ricciarda. I have not yet given you absolution.

Marquise Keep talking. It is not entirely certain that I want it.

Cardinal Beware, Marquise! If you want to challenge me you had better have solid armor, without any chinks. I am not trying to threaten you. I have nothing more to say to you. Find another confessor. *(Exit.)*

Marquise That was incredible. He went out with his fists clenched! His eyes were ablaze with anger! To talk of "experienced hands," of "a direction to give certain things"! Hah! Why, what does that mean? I can imagine that he might want to find out my secrets and tell my husband. But if that is not his aim, what does he want to make of me? The Duke's mistress? "To know everything and guide everything," he said! That cannot be. There is some other more somber and inexplicable mystery behind it. Cibo would not enter into such a business. No, that is sure, I know him. That would be fit for a Lorenzaccio, but for him! He must have some broader and deeper hidden idea. Oh, it is frightening how men suddenly reveal themselves after ten years' silence!

What shall I do now? Do I love Alessandro? No, I do not love him, no, definitely not. I said I did not in my confession and I was not lying. Why is Lorenzo in Massa? Why is the Duke so insistent with me? Why did I answer that I would not see him any more? Why? Oh, why is there a magnet, an inexplicable charm in all this that draws me on? *(She opens her window.)*

How beautiful you are, Florence; but how sad! There is more than one house that Alessandro has entered at night, wrapped in his cloak. He is a rake, I know it.—And why should you be entangled in all this, Florence? Who is it that I love, then, you or him?

Agnolo *(entering)* Madam, His Highness has just come into the courtyard.

Marquise How strange! That Malaspina has left me shaking.

Scene 4.

The Soderini palace.

(Maria Soderini, Caterina, Lorenzo seated.)

Caterina *(holding a book)* What story shall I read you, mother?

Maria My little Kate is making fun of her poor mother. You know I can't understand a thing in those Latin books of yours.

Caterina This one is not in Latin at all, although it was translated from it. It is the history of Rome.

Lorenzo I know a lot about Roman history. Once upon a time there was a young gentleman named Tarquin junior.[36]

Caterina Oh, that is a bloody story.

Lorenzo Not at all. It is a fairy-tale. Brutus was nothing but a madman with a one-track mind. Tarquin was a Duke[37] full of wisdom who would go in his bedroom slippers to see if little girls were fast asleep.

Caterina So you speak ill of Lucretia?

Lorenzo She allowed herself the pleasure of sin and the glory of death. She let herself be taken alive like a lark in a trap and then she very nicely slipped her little knife into her belly.

Maria You may feel nothing but contempt for women but why do you make a point of belittling them to your mother and your sister?

Lorenzo I hold you both in esteem. Apart from that, the world is abhorrent to me.

Maria Do you[38] know what I dreamed last night, my child?

Lorenzo What?

Maria It was not really a dream, since I was not asleep. I was all alone in this great room; my lamp was far away, on that table there near the window. I was thinking of the days when I was happy, the days when you were a child, my Lorenzino. I was looking out into the dark night and saying to myself: he won't be coming home until daylight, he who used to spend nights working. My eyes filled with tears and I shook my head when I felt them flowing. All at once I heard someone walking in the gallery. I turned around; a man dressed in black came up to me with a book under his arm: it was you, Renzo. "See how early you have come home," I cried. But the ghost sat down next to the lamp without answering; he opened his book and I recognized my Lorenzino of former times.

Lorenzo You saw it?

Maria As I am seeing you.

Lorenzo When did it leave?

Maria When you rang the bell this morning as you came in.

Lorenzo My own ghost! And it went away when I came home?

Maria It stood up with a melancholy air, and disappeared like a morning vapor.

Lorenzo Caterina, Caterina, read me the story of Brutus.[39]

Caterina What is the matter with you? You are trembling all over.

Lorenzo Mother, this evening sit where you were last night and, if my ghost reappears, tell it that it will soon see something that will astonish it. *(A knock is heard.)*

Caterina It is uncle Bindo, with Battista Venturi. *(Enter Bindo and Venturi.)*

Bindo *(softly, to Maria)* I have come to make one last attempt.

Maria We shall leave you alone. I wish you success! *(Exit, with Caterina.)*

Bindo Lorenzo, why do you not deny this scandalous story that is being told about you?

Lorenzo What story?

Bindo They are saying that you fainted at the sight of a sword.

Lorenzo Do you believe it, uncle?

Bindo I have seen you fence in Rome. But I would not be surprised if the life you lead here was making you more cowardly than a dog.

Lorenzo The story is true: I did faint. Hello, Venturi. What price is your merchandise bringing? How is business going?

Venturi My lord, I run a silk factory; but it is an insult to call me a merchant.

Lorenzo That is true. I only meant that, when you were in school, you developed the harmless practice of selling silk.

Bindo I have confided in signor Venturi the plans that are currently absorbing so many families in Florence. He is a worthy friend of freedom, and I expect you[40] to treat him as such, Lorenzo. The time for jokes is past. You have told us several times that the extreme confidence the Duke has in you is just a trap that you are setting. Is that true or false? Are you with us or aren't you? That is what we must know. All the great families see clearly that the Medici's despotism is neither just nor bearable. By what right should we allow that proud house to rise in peace over the ruins of our privileges? The treaty is not being observed. Germany's power is making itself felt more and more absolutely each day. It is time to put an end to that and to assemble the patriots. Will you answer this appeal?

Lorenzo What do you have to say, signor Venturi? Speak up, speak up, my uncle is catching his breath. Seize this opportunity, if you love your country.

Venturi My lord, I agree completely, and have not a single word to add.

Lorenzo Not a word? Not a fine little resounding word? You do not know what true eloquence is. You spin a grand phrase around a fine little word, neither too long nor too short, as round as a top. You throw your left arm back so as to drape your cloak in folds full of dignity tempered with grace. You utter your phrase, which unwinds like a droning cord, and the little top whirls off with a delightful hum. You could almost pick it up in the palm of your hand, like children in the street.

Bindo What insolence! Answer me or I shall leave at once.

Lorenzo I am with you, uncle. Can you not see by my haircut that I am for the republic to the very core? Just see the way my beard is trimmed. Do not have a moment's doubt: love of country permeates my innermost garments.[41] *(A ringing is heard at the gate; the courtyard fills with pages and horses.)*

A page *(entering)* The Duke. *(Enter Alessandro.)*

Lorenzo My prince, your favor is too great! You deign to visit a poor servant in person?

Duke Who are those men? I have to talk with you.

Lorenzo I have the honor of introducing to Your Highness my uncle, Bindo Altoviti, who regrets that his lengthy stay in Naples has prevented him from throwing himself at your feet before now. The other gentleman is the illustrious Battista Venturi, who manufactures silk it is true, but does not sell any. May the unexpected presence of so great a prince in this lowly house not disturb you, my dear uncle, nor you either, worthy Venturi. What you ask for will be granted to you or else you will be entitled to say that my supplications have no credit with my gracious sovereign.

Duke What do you request, Bindo?

Bindo Your Highness, I am terribly sorry if my nephew…

Lorenzo The title of ambassador to Rome belongs to no one at the moment. My uncle went so far as to hope to obtain it by your kindness. There is not a single man in Florence who can bear comparison with him when it comes to the devotion and respect due to the Medici family.

Duke Is that true, Renzino? Well, my dear Bindo, so be it. Come to the palace tomorrow morning.

Bindo Your Highness, I am overwhelmed! How can I show...

Lorenzo Signor Venturi here, although he never sells any silk, requests a privilege for his mills.

Duke What privilege?

Lorenzo Your arms over the door along with the ducal warrant. Grant it to him, my lord, if you love those who love you.

Duke Then it will be done. Is that all? Go on, gentlemen, peace be with you.

Venturi Your Highness!... Your goodness overwhelms me... I cannot express...

Duke *(to his guards)* Let these two men through.

Bindo *(going out, softly to Venturi)* What a dastardly trick.

Venturi *(as above)* What are you going to do?

Bindo *(as above)* What the devil can I do? I have been nominated.

Venturi *(as above)* This is terrible. *(Exeunt.)*

Duke The Cibo woman is mine.

Lorenzo I am sorry to hear it.

Duke Why?

Lorenzo Because that will make the others look bad.

Duke Why, not really, she already bores me. Tell me, darling, who can that beautiful woman be, arranging those flowers at that window? I keep seeing her every time I pass by.

Lorenzo Where do you mean?

Duke Over there, on the other side, in the palace.

Lorenzo Oh, that is nothing.

Duke Nothing? Do you call those arms "nothing"? What a Venus, by the devil's guts!

Lorenzo She is a neighbor.

Duke I should like to speak with that neighbor. Hah! by God, unless I am mistaken, that is Caterina Ginori.

Lorenzo No.

Duke I recognize her quite well. She is your aunt. Damnation, I had forgotten that face. Bring her over for supper.

Lorenzo That would be very difficult. She is a paragon of virtue.

Duke Come now! Do any of those exist for people like us?

Lorenzo I shall ask her, if you wish. But I warn you, she is a pedant. She speaks Latin.

Duke That is all right, she does not make love in Latin. Come on over here; we can see her better from this gallery.

Lorenzo Some other time, darling.—Right now I have no time to waste:—I have to go to Strozzi's.[42]

Duke What, that old fool's house?

Lorenzo Yes, that old wretch, that scoundrel's house. He cannot seem to cure himself of the peculiar folly of opening his purse to all those base creatures called exiles, and those beggars meet every day at his house before donning their shoes and taking up their staffs. Now, my intent is to go as soon as possible and have dinner with the old gallows' bait and renew the assurance of my heartfelt friendship to him. I shall have some good story to tell you this evening, some charming little escapade that will make a few of all those rabble get up early tomorrow morning.

Duke I am so lucky to have you, darling! I confess that I do not understand how they can receive you.

Lorenzo Hah! If you only knew how easy it is to lie impudently to the very face of a boor! It just shows that you have never tried. By the way, did you not tell me that you wanted to give your portrait to someone or other? I have a painter I shall bring you. He is a protégé of mine.

Duke All right, all right; but don't forget your aunt. She is why I came to see you. The devil take me, you have an aunt who really appeals to me.

Lorenzo What about the Cibo woman?

Duke I tell you to speak to your aunt about me. *(Exeunt.)*

Scene 5.

A room in the Strozzi palace.
(Filippo Strozzi, the Prior, Luisa embroidering, Lorenzo lying on a sofa.)

Filippo God forbid anything should happen! So many undying, implacable hatreds have begun just this way! A word! The vapor from dinner prattling over some debauchee's lips, and suddenly families are at war and knives are drawn. You are insulted, so you kill; you have killed, so you are killed. Soon hatred takes root, sons are rocked in the coffins of their forefathers, and whole generations issue forth from the earth with sword in hand.

Prior Perhaps it was wrong of me to recall that nasty speech and that cursed trip to Monteoliveto. But how can one endure these Salviati?

Filippo Oh, Leone, Leone, I ask you, what difference would it make for Luisa and for ourselves if you had said nothing to my children? Cannot a Strozzi's virtue ignore the words of a Salviati? Does one who dwells in a marble palace have to know of the obscenities that commoners scribble on its walls? What do Giuliano's words matter? Won't my daughter find a proper husband all the same?[43] Will her children respect her the less? Will I, her father, recall any of that as I give her a good-night kiss? What have we come to if the insolence of the first man who comes along draws swords such as ours from their scabbards? Now all is lost: Piero is furious about what you told us. He has launched a campaign; he has gone to see the Pazzi. God knows what will happen! If he meets Salviati, blood will be shed—mine, my own blood, on the cobblestones of Florence! Oh, why did I become a father?

Prior If someone had reported a comment about my sister to me, whatever it might be, I would have turned my back and it would have all stopped right there. But that one was addressed to me. It was so vulgar that I imagined the boor did not know who he was talking about.—But he knew only too well.

Filippo Yes, they know, the scoundrels! They know very well where they are striking! The old tree is made of too solid wood; they would not dare try to cut into it. But they know the delicate fiber that quivers inside it when its frailest bud is attacked. My Luisa! Oh, what is reason, then? My hands tremble just to think of it. Good God! Is reason nothing but old age?

Prior Piero is too violent.

Filippo Poor Piero! Did you see how red his face grew! How he shuddered on hearing you tell of that insult to his sister! *I* am the madman: I should not have let you go on. Piero paced from one end of the room to the other, restless, out of his mind with rage;—he walked back and forth as I am doing now. I watched him in silence: what a splendid sight it is to see pure blood rising in an untainted brow! Oh, fatherland, I thought, here is one and he is my eldest. Oh, Leone, I cannot help it, I am a Strozzi.

Prior Perhaps the danger is not so great as you think.—It is very unlikely he would encounter Salviati this evening.—Tomorrow we shall all look on this with greater wisdom.

Filippo Have no doubt: Piero will kill him or he will be killed. *(He opens the window.)* Where are they now? Night is falling; the city is plunged into deep shadow; those dark streets terrify me;—there is blood flowing somewhere, I am sure of it.

Prior Calm down.

Filippo The way Piero rushed out, I am sure he will come home either avenged or dead. I saw him take down his sword with a frown on his face. He was biting his lips and the muscles in his arms were as taut as a bow. Yes, yes, at this moment he is either dying or he is avenged, there is no doubt about it.

Prior Get hold of yourself, close that window.

Filippo Well, then, Florence, teach the color of my noble blood to your cobblestones! Forty of your sons have it in their veins. And I, as chief of this vast family, will lean my gray head out of these windows many a time again in paternal anguish! Many a time the blood you may be indifferently drinking at this very moment will dry in the sunshine on your squares. But do not laugh tonight at old Strozzi, who fears for his child. Be sparing of his family, for the day will come when you will count its numbers, when you will come to the window with him and when your heart will beat, too, as you hear the clash of our swords.

Luisa Father! Father! You frighten me.

Prior *(softly, to Luisa)* Isn't that Tommaso prowling around under those lanterns? I thought I recognized him by his short stature. Now he is gone.

Filippo My poor city! Fathers like me are waiting all over for the return of their children! My poor country! My poor country! There are many others at this moment who have taken up their cloaks and swords to plunge into that dark night. And those who wait for them are not uneasy, they know that they will starve tomorrow if they do not freeze to death tonight. And we wait, in these sumptuous palaces, to be insulted before drawing our swords! A drunkard's words move us to rage and scatter our sons and friends through these dark streets! But public misfortunes do not shake the dust from our weapons. Filippo Strozzi is considered a decent man because he does good without preventing evil. And now, as a father, what would I not give for there to be some person in the world who could give me back my son and punish by trial the insult to my daughter? But why should anyone prevent the evil that falls to me when I have not prevented what befalls others, though I had the power to. I have bent over my books and dreamed of what I admired in antiquity for my country. The walls around me cried out for vengeance, and I stopped my ears in order to plunge deeper into my meditations. Tyranny had to come and strike me in the face, to rouse me to say: "Let us act!" And my vengeance has gray hair. *(Enter Piero, Tommaso, and Francesco Pazzi.)*

Piero It is done. Salviati is dead. *(He embraces his sister.)*

Luisa How dreadful! You are covered with blood.

Piero We waited for him at the corner of the Via degli Arcieri. Francesco stopped his horse, Tommaso struck him in the leg, and I…

Luisa Be still! Be still! You make me shudder. Your eyes are starting from their sockets; your hands are horrid; your entire body is shaking and you are as pale as death.

Lorenzo *(rising)* How handsome you are, Piero. You are as grand as vengeance.

Piero Who says so? What are you doing here, Lorenzaccio? *(He goes to his father.)* When are you going to shut your door to that wretch? Don't you know what kind of man he is, not to mention the story of his duel with Maurizio?

Filippo That is enough. I know all that. If Lorenzo is here, it is because I have good reasons for letting him in. We shall discuss it at the proper time and place.

Piero *(muttering under his breath)* Hum? Reasons for letting that scoundrel in! I could very well find some for pushing him out the window one of these days. Say what you will, I am suffocating in this room to see a scab like him lounging about in our seats.

Filippo Come now, be still! You are a hot-head. Please God your actions this evening have no ill consequences for us! The first thing you must do is hide.

Piero Hide! By all the saints, why should I hide?

Lorenzo *(to Tommaso)* So, you struck him on the shoulder?... Now just tell me... *(He draws him toward a window; the two go on speaking quietly.)*

Piero No, father, I shall not hide. The insult was made in public, right in the middle of the town square. I struck him down in the middle of the street and it is fitting for me to tell it to the whole city tomorrow morning. Since when do people have to hide because they have avenged their honor? I would be happy to walk around with my drawn sword and not wipe a drop of blood from it.

Filippo Come over here, I have to speak with you. You weren't wounded, my child? You weren't hurt during all that? *(Exeunt.)*

Scene 6.

The Duke's palace.

(The Duke, half undressed; Tebaldeo, painting his portrait; Giomo, playing the guitar.)

Giomo *(singing)*

When I die, oh Ganymede,
Take my heart to my beloved.
The devil take the funeral mass,
The priests and all their prayers.

Tears are nothing but clear water;
Tell her to open up a keg of wine;
Let them sing a chorus on my coffin;
I'll answer back from in my tomb.

Duke I knew I had something I wanted to ask you. Tell me, Giomo, what had that fellow done to you, the one I saw you battering so joyously a while ago?

Giomo By God, I couldn't tell you, nor could he.

Duke Why? Is he dead?

Giomo It was a young fellow from one of the houses nearby. A moment ago, as I went by, I thought I saw them burying him.

Duke When my Giomo strikes, he strikes hard.

Giomo That is all right for you to say. I have seen you kill a man with a blow more than once.

Duke Do you think so? I must have been drunk. When I have had just enough to get tipsy, all my slightest blows are lethal. Whatever is the matter, lad? Is your hand shaking? You have an awful look on your face.

Tebaldeo It is nothing, my lord, if it please Your Highness. *(Enter Lorenzo.)*

Lorenzo How is it going? Are you happy with my protégé? *(He picks up the Duke's coat of mail from the sofa.)* You have a pretty coat of mail, darling! But it must be very hot.

Duke In truth, if it bothered me I wouldn't wear it. But it is made of steel wire. The sharpest file could not bite into one of its links and at the same time it is as light as silk. There is probably nothing like it in all of Europe; so I hardly ever take it off, practically never.

Lorenzo It is very light, but very solid. Do you think it would stop a dagger?

Duke I am sure of it.

Lorenzo Now that I think of it, that is true. You always wear it under your doublet. The other day, at the hunt, I was riding pillion behind you and as I clasped your body, I could quite definitely feel it. That is a wise habit.

Duke It is not that I distrust anyone. As you say, it is a habit—just a soldier's habit.

Lorenzo Your clothes are marvelous. What a scent in these gloves! Why in the world are you posing half-dressed? This coat of mail would have been very effective in your portrait. You were wrong to take it off.

Duke It is the painter who wanted it. It is always better, in any case, to pose with one's chest exposed: look at the ancients.

Lorenzo Where the devil is my guitar? I must sing harmony with Giomo. *(Exit.)*

Tebaldeo Your Highness, I won't paint any more today.

Giomo *(by the window)* What can Lorenzo be doing? Look at him gazing into the well in the middle of the garden. I don't think he should be looking for his guitar there.

Duke Give me my clothes. Where in the world is my coat of mail?

Giomo I cannot find it. I have looked all over but it has disappeared.

Duke Renzino was holding it just a few minutes ago. He must have thrown it into a corner as he went out, as lazy fellows do.

Giomo It is unbelievable. Your coat of mail is nowhere to be found.

Duke Come now, you are dreaming! That is impossible.

Giomo Look for yourself, your Highness. The room is not all that big.

Duke Renzo was holding it there on that sofa. *(Lorenzo comes back.)* What ever have you done with my coat of mail? We cannot find it.

Lorenzo I put it back where it was. Wait; no; I put it down on that chair; no, it was on the bed. I don't know. But I did find my guitar. *(He sings, accompanying himself.)*

Good morning, Mother Superior...

Giomo In the garden well, evidently... Because you were leaning over it a little while ago, apparently deep in thought.

Lorenzo My greatest pleasure is spitting into wells to make circles. Apart from drinking and sleeping, I do nothing else. *(He goes on playing.)*

Good morning, good morning, Mother Superior my love.

Duke It is extraordinary for that coat to have gotten lost! I do not think I have taken it off twice in my life, except when I go to bed.

Lorenzo Forget about it. You are not going to make a chambermaid out of the son of a Pope, are you? Your servants will find it.

Duke The devil take you! You are the one who lost it.

Lorenzo If I were the Duke of Florence, I would be worried about more than my coats of mail. By the way, I have talked about you to my dear aunt.[44] Everything is absolutely fine. Come on and sit over here so I can whisper to you.

Giomo *(softly, to the Duke)* That is strange, to say the least. The coat of mail has been stolen.

Duke We shall find it. *(He sits down next to Lorenzo.)*

Giomo *(aside)* It just is not natural to leave the company to go and spit in a well. I would like to find that coat of mail just to rid my mind of an old idea that keeps returning. Bah! That Lorenzaccio! The coat must be lying under a chair.

Scene 7.

In front of the palace.

(Enter Salviati, covered with blood and limping; two men are holding him up.)

Salviati *(shouting)* Alessandro de' Medici, open your window and just see how they treat your servants.

Duke *(at the window)* Who is that in the mud? Who is clinging to my palace walls and shouting so horribly?

Salviati The Strozzi have murdered me. I am going to die at your door.

Duke Which of the Strozzi and why?

Salviati Just because I said their sister was in love with you, my noble Duke. The Strozzi considered their sister insulted because I said that she liked you. Three of them attacked me. I recognized Piero and Tommaso; I do not know the third one.

Duke Have them bring you up here. By Hercules, the murderers will spend the night in prison and we shall hang them tomorrow morning. *(Salviati enters the palace.)*

ACT THREE
Scene 1.

Lorenzo's bedroom.

(Lorenzo and Scoronconcolo, fencing.)

Scoronc. Master, have you had enough of the game?

Lorenzo No. Shout louder. Here, parry this one! Now you shall die! Take this, you wretch!

Scoronc. Murder! He is killing me! He is cutting my throat!

Lorenzo Die! Die! Die! Come on now, stamp your feet.

Scoronc. Help, archers! Come to my aid! He is killing me! Damned Lorenzo!

Lorenzo Die, you villain! I shall drain your blood, you pig, I shall bleed you white. Right to the heart, he is disemboweled.—Come on now, shout, stamp your foot, kill him! Slit his belly open! Let's cut him up in pieces and eat them, eat them! I am in it up to my elbow. Dig into his throat, roll him over, roll him! Let's bite into him, bite, bite! *(He falls exhausted.)*

Scoronc. *(wiping his brow)* This is a rough game you have invented, master. You play it like a real tiger. Thunder and damnation, you roar like a cave full of panthers and lions.

Lorenzo Oh, day of blood, oh my wedding day! Oh, sun, sun! You have been as dry as dust for long enough; you are dying of thirst, sun! His blood will make you drunk. Oh, my revenge! Your fingernails have been growing for such a long time! Oh, Ugolino,[45] your teeth must gnaw the skull, the skull!

Scoronc. Are you delirious? Do you have a fever, or are you a dream yourself?

Lorenzo The coward, the coward,—the pimp,—the little skinny one, the fathers, the daughters,—farewells, endless farewells,—the banks of the Arno echoing with farewells!—Children write it on the walls;—Laugh, old man, laugh in your white cap,—don't you see that my nails are growing? —Oh, the skull, the skull! *(He faints.)*

Scoronc. Master, you have an enemy. *(He throws water on his face.)* Come on, master, it is not worth thrashing about so. You either have higher feelings or you don't. I shall never forget that you obtained a certain pardon for me, without which I would be far from here now. Master, if you have an enemy, tell me and I'll get rid of him for you without anyone noticing.

Lorenzo It is nothing. I tell you, my only pleasure is frightening my neighbors.

Scoronc. We have been stamping around in this room and knocking everything topsy-turvy for so long, they must have grown pretty used to our noise.[46] I think you could slit thirty men's throats in this corridor and roll them around on your floor without anyone in the house noticing anything new has happened. If you want to frighten your neighbors, that's not the way to do it. They were frightened the first time, it is true. But now they just curse and they don't even bother to leave their seats or open their windows.

Lorenzo Do you think so?

Scoronc. You have an enemy, master. Haven't I seen you stamp your feet and curse the day you were born? Don't I have ears? And in the midst of your ranting, haven't I distinctly heard one clear little word: revenge? Come now, master, believe me, you are wasting away;—you no longer have a sense of humor like you used to[47]; believe me, there is nothing as hard to digest as a good hate. For every two men under the sun, isn't there always one whose shadow annoys the other? Your cure is here in my scabbard; let me heal you. *(He draws his sword.)*

Lorenzo Has that cure ever worked for you?

Scoronc. Four or five times. One day in Padua, a young lady was telling me...

Lorenzo Show me that sword. Oh, my lad, that is a fine blade.

Scoronc. Just try it and you'll see.

Lorenzo You have guessed my problem,—I have an enemy. But I shall not use a sword on him that has already been used for others. The one that kills him will have only one baptism here on earth; it will take his name.

Scoronc. What is the man's name?

Lorenzo What does it matter? Are you devoted to me?

Scoronc. I would put Christ back up on the cross for you.

Lorenzo I am telling you this in confidence,—I shall do the deed in this room. Listen carefully and make no mistake. If I slaughter him with the first blow, don't try to touch him. But I am no bigger than a flea and he is a wild boar. If he fights back, I shall count on you to hold his hands. Nothing else, do you hear? He belongs to me. I shall inform you at the right time and place.

Scoronc. Amen!

Scene 2.

The Strozzi palace.

(Enter Filippo and Piero.)

Piero When I think of it, I feel like cutting off my right hand. To think I missed out with that scoundrel! Such a clear-cut blow, and to think I bungled it! There is no one who would not have benefitted if people had been able to say: There is one less Salviati in the streets. But the rascal acted like a spider—he fell down and folded up his crooked legs, and he played dead, for fear of being finished off.

Filippo What does it matter to you if he is alive? Your vengeance is all the more complete.

Piero Yes, I know. That is how you see things. Look here, father, you are a good patriot but an even better father. Do not get involved in all this.

Filippo What are you thinking of now? Can't you go for a quarter of an hour without planning some mischief?

Piero No, by the devil, I cannot live quietly for a quarter of an hour in this poisoned air. The sky weighs down on my head like a prison vault and I feel as if I am breathing in jeers and drunkards' hiccups in the streets. Good-bye, I have some business to do now.

Filippo Where are you going?

Piero Why do you want to know? I am going to the Pazzi's.

Filippo Then wait for me, for I am going there, too.

Piero Not right now, father, this is not the right time for you.

Filippo Be frank with me.

Piero This is between us. There are about fifty of us there, the Rucellai and others, who cannot stand the bastard's guts.

Filippo And so?

Piero And so avalanches are sometimes started by a pebble no bigger than your fingernail.

Filippo But you don't have anything set? No plan? No measures taken? Oh, what children you are! You are playing with life and death! Questions that have stirred up the world! Ideas that have turned thousands of heads gray and made them roll like grains of sand onto executioners' feet! Plans that divine Providence itself looks on at in silence and terror, and whose consummation it leaves to men, not daring to get involved! You talk about all that as you fence and drink your glass of Spanish wine, just as if it were a horse or a masquerade! Do you know what a republic is? The craftsman deep in his workshop, the plowman in his field, the very life of a kingdom? Men's happiness, God of justice! Oh, what children! Can you count on your fingers?

Piero A good cut of a scalpel cures all ills.

Filippo Cure! Cure! Do you know that even the slightest scalpel cut must be given by a doctor? Do you know that it takes life-long experience, knowledge as great as the world, to draw a drop of blood from the arm of a patient? Was I not also offended last night when you hid your naked sword under your cloak? Am I not Luisa's father as you are her brother? Was that not a just revenge? And yet, do you know how much it cost me? Oh, fathers know that, but not their children. If you are a father some day, we shall speak of it.

Piero You know how to love; you ought to know how to hate.

Filippo What have those Pazzi[48] done to God? They invite their friends to come and plot as you invite people to play dice, and their friends slip on their forefathers' blood as they enter their courtyard. What makes their swords so thirsty? What do you want, then, what do you want?

Piero Why are you denying your own words? Have I not heard you say what we are saying a hundred times over? Do we not know what is troubling you when your servants awaken to see your windows bright with the previous night's torches? Those who spend sleepless nights do not die quietly.

Filippo What are you driving at? Answer me.

Piero The Medici are a plague. A man bitten by a snake has no need of doctors. He has to cauterize his wound.

Filippo And when you have overthrown what exists, what will you put in its place?

Piero At least we are sure we won't find anything worse.

Filippo I have told you, count on your fingers.

Piero A hydra's heads are easy to count.

Filippo So you want to do something? Is that definite?

Piero We want to cut the murderers of Florence down.

Filippo Is it irrevocable? You want to take action?

Piero Good-bye, father. Let me go alone.

Filippo Since when does the old eagle remain in his nest while the eaglets go out to hunt? Oh, my children, my fine, brave young ones! You have the strength that I have lost, you are today what young Filippo used to be; let him have grown old for you! Take me with you, son, I see that you want to take action. I shall not make any long speeches to you, I shall only say a few words. There may be something worth while in this gray head: a few words and that will be all. I am not yet a dotard. I shall not be a burden to you. Do not leave without me, my son. Wait until I get my cloak.

Piero Come, my noble father. We shall kiss the hem of your robe. You are our patriarch, come and see the dreams of your life marching in the sunlight. Freedom is ripe; come, old gardener of Florence, come see the plant you love spring forth from the earth. *(Exeunt.)*

Scene 3.

A street.

(A German officer and some soldiers, with Tommaso Strozzi in their midst.)

Officer If we do not find him at his house, we shall find him at the Pazzi's.

Tommaso Go right ahead and do not worry. You will see how much it costs.

Officer No threats: I am executing the Duke's orders and I do not have to take anything from anyone.

Tommaso You imbecile! How can you arrest a Strozzi on a Medici's orders! *(A group forms around them.)*

A burgher Why are you arresting that gentleman? We know him well: he is Filippo's son.

Another Let him go. We shall answer for him.

First b. Yes, yes, we can answer for the Strozzi. Let him go, or you'll get your ears boxed.

Officer Get going, you rabble! Let the Duke's justice pass, if you do not want to feel our pikes. *(Piero and Filippo arrive.)*

Piero What is going on? Why all this noise? What are you doing here, Tommaso?

First b. Stop him, Filippo. He is trying to take your son to prison.

Filippo To prison? On whose order?

Piero To prison? Do you know who you are dealing with?

Officer Seize that man. *(The soldiers arrest Piero.)*

Piero Let go of me, you wretches, or I shall cut you open like pigs!

Filippo On whose order are you acting, sir?

Officer *(showing the Duke's order)* Here is my warrant. I have an order to arrest Piero and Tommaso Strozzi. *(The soldiers push back the people, who throw stones at them.)*

Piero What are we accused of? What have we done? Help me, friends. Let us thrash these scoundrels. *(He draws his sword. Another detachment of soldiers arrives.)*

Officer Come over here and give me a hand. *(Piero is disarmed.)* Forward, march! The first man who comes too close will get a pike in his belly! That will teach them to mind their own business.

Piero No on has the right to arrest me without an order from the Council of Eight.[49] A lot I care for Alessandro's orders! Where is the Council of Eight's order?

Officer We are taking you to appear before them.

Piero If I am to appear before them, I can say nothing. What am I accused of?

Commoner What, Filippo, are you going to allow your sons to be taken before the court of the Eight!

Piero Answer me, what am I accused of?

Officer That is not my concern. *(The soldiers exit with Piero and Tommaso.)*

Piero *(as he leaves)* Don't worry, father. The Eight will send me back home for supper and the bastard will have to pay court charges.

Filippo *(alone, sitting down on a bench)* I have many children but not for long, if this happens so quickly. What in the world have we come to if an act of revenge, as just as the sky above is clear, is punished as a crime! What, the two eldest children of a family as old as the city, imprisoned like highway robbers! The grossest of insults is avenged, a Salviati is struck down, merely struck down, and soldiers are sent for! Out of your scabbard then, my sword. If the sacred judiciary apparatus becomes a shield for pimps and drunkards, let the ax and the dagger, the weapon of murderers, protect decent men. Oh, Christ, that justice should have become a panderer! The honor of the Strozzi outraged in public and a tribunal answering for a churl's jeers! A Salviati flings his wine- and blood-stained gauntlet at the noblest family in Florence and when he is punished draws an executioner's ax to defend himself! By the light of the sun, I spoke less than a quarter hour ago against the idea of revolt, and this is the way they reward me, with my words of peace on my lips! Come and move, my arms, and you, old body bent with age and study, rise up and take action! *(Enter Lorenzo.)*

Lorenzo Are you begging for alms, Filippo, sitting there on the street-corner?

Filippo I am asking men's justice for alms. I am a beggar famished for justice and my honor is in tatters.

Lorenzo What change is going to come over the world, and what new dress will nature don, if the mask of anger has settled on the august, peaceable face of old Filippo? Oh, father, what are these complaints? For whom are you shedding those most precious jewels under the sun, the tears of an undaunted, blameless man?

Filippo We must be rid of the Medici, Lorenzo. You yourself are a Medici, but only in name. If I have really grown to know you, if the dreadful role you have been playing has found an impassive and faithful spectator in me, now let the man emerge from the play-actor. If you have ever been anything decent, be so today. Piero and Tommaso are in jail.

Lorenzo Yes, yes, I know that.

Filippo Is that your answer? Is that your true face, man without a sword?

Lorenzo What is it you want? Tell me and then you shall have my answer.

Filippo Action! I don't know how. I cannot yet know what means to employ, what lever to set under that citadel of death to pry it up and push it into the river, what course to take, what men I should go and get. But action, action, action! Oh, Lorenzo, the time has come. Are you not denigrated, labeled a dog and a coward? If I have kept my door, my hand, my heart open to you, speak, let me see if I was wrong. Have you not spoken to me of a man who is also named Lorenzo, hiding behind the one before me? Does that man not love his country, is he not devoted to his friends? You said so, and I believed it. Speak out, speak out, the time has come.

Lorenzo If I am not such as you desire, may the sun fall down on my head.

Filippo My friend, it brings bad luck to laugh at a desperate old man. If you are telling the truth, you must act! I have promises from you that would commit God Himself, and it was on those promises that I welcomed you. The role you have been playing is a filthy, loathsome one, one that the prodigal son would not have played in a day of madness, and yet I welcomed you. When the very stones cried out as you went by, when each of your steps made human blood splash up, I called you by the holy name of friend. I have let myself be deaf in order to believe you, blind in order to love you. I have allowed the shadow of your evil reputation to darken my honor, and my children have doubted me, finding the horrible traces of your hand on mine. Be a decent man, since I have; take action, for you are young and I am old.

Lorenzo Piero and Tommaso are in jail. Is that all?

Filippo God in heaven, yes, that is all! Practically nothing: two children of my loins who have gone to sit on the thieves' bench. Two heads that I have kissed as many times as I have gray hairs and that I will find nailed to the door of the fortress tomorrow morning. Yes, that is all, nothing more in truth.

Lorenzo Don't speak to me like that. I am gnawed by a sadness compared to which the darkest night is a dazzling light. *(He sits down next to Filippo.)*

Filippo It is not possible for me to let my children die, don't you see? Even if they were to rip off my arms and legs, the mutilated pieces of Filippo would join together again like a snake and rise up for vengeance. I know all that so well! The Council of Eight! a tribunal of stone men! a forest of specters over which the dismal wind of doubt blows from time to time and stirs them up for a moment, only to resolve itself into a word without appeal. A word, a word, oh conscience! Those men eat, they sleep, they have wives and daughters! Oh, let them kill and let them slaughter; but not my children, not my children.

Lorenzo Piero is a man. He will speak, and he will be set free.

Filippo Oh, my Piero, my first-born!

Lorenzo Go back home, remain calm, or even better, leave Florence. I will take care of everything, if you leave Florence.

Filippo What, me, an exile! In a strange bed at my final hour! Oh, God, all that because of something said by a Salviati.

Lorenzo Let me tell you: Salviati wanted to seduce your daughter but not just for himself. Alessandro has a foot in that man's bed. He exercises *droit du seigneur* in it over prostitution.

Filippo And we should do nothing! Oh, Lorenzo, Lorenzo, you are a steadfast man. Speak to me, I am weak and my heart is too involved in all this. I have lost my strength, you see; I have spent too much time thinking, I have gone round and round like the horse turning a wine-press. I am not worth anything for battle any more. Tell me what you think and I shall do it.

Lorenzo Go back to your house, my good sir.

Filippo I know what I shall do: I shall go to the Pazzi's. There are fifty young men there, all full of resolve. They have sworn to take action. I shall speak nobly to them, as a Strozzi and a father, and they will listen to me. This evening I shall invite the forty members of my family to supper and tell them what has happened to me. We shall see! We shall see! Nothing is decided yet. Let the Medici beware! Farewell, I am going to the Pazzi's. I was on my way there with Piero when he was arrested.

Lorenzo There are a number of demons, Filippo. The one that is tempting you at this moment is not the least of all to be feared.

Filippo What do you mean?

Lorenzo Beware; it is a demon more beautiful than the angel Gabriel: freedom, the fatherland, mankind's happiness—all those words resound at his approach like the strings of a harp, it is the sound of the silver scales of his flaming wings. The tears from his eyes impregnate the earth, and he holds the martyr's palm in his hand. His words purify the air around his lips. His flight is so swift that none may say where he is bound. Beware! Once in my life I saw him soar across the skies. I was bent over my books; the touch of his hand made my hair quiver, as light as a feather. Whether I listened to him or not I would rather not say.

Filippo I can scarcely understand what you are saying, and I do not know why but I am afraid to.

Lorenzo Is that all you have in mind: to free your sons? Look me in the eye: is some other thought, more vast and terrible, not drawing you like a thundering chariot into the midst of those young men?

Filippo Why, yes, let the injustice done to my family be a signal for freedom. For me and for all, I shall go!

Lorenzo Beware, Filippo, you have thought of the happiness of humanity.

Filippo What do you mean? Are you a filthy vapor, the same inside as outside? Is that what you contain? You told me of a precious liquor whose vessel you were.

Lorenzo Indeed, I am precious to you, for I shall kill Alessandro.

Filippo You?

Lorenzo Yes, I, tomorrow or the day after. Go back home, try and get your children freed. If you can't, let them suffer a slight penalty. I know for certain that there is no other danger to them and I swear to you that within a few days there will be no more Alessandro de' Medici in Florence than there is sunshine at midnight.

Filippo Even if that were true, why would it be wrong of me to think of freedom? Won't it come when you have struck your blow, if you do?

Lorenzo Filippo, Filippo, beware. You have sixty years of virtue on your gray head. That is too high a stake to gamble with.

Filippo If you are hiding something that I can understand under those somber words, speak up. You are strangely provoking.

Lorenzo Such as you see me, Filippo, I once was a decent man. I believed in virtue, in man's nobility, as a martyr believes in his God. I shed more tears over poor Italy than Niobe over her daughters.

Filippo And so, Lorenzo?

Lorenzo My youth was as pure as gold. During twenty years of silence, a storm built up in my breast, and I must really be a spark of lightning, because all of a sudden, on one particular night when

I was sitting in the ruins of the ancient Coliseum, for some unknown reason I stood up, I raised my dew-drenched arms toward heaven, and I swore that one of my country's tyrants would die by my hand. I was a peaceable student, I was concerned then with nothing but the arts and sciences and I am unable to say how that strange oath arose in me. Perhaps that is what men feel when they fall in love.

Filippo I have always had confidence in you, and yet I feel as if I were dreaming.

Lorenzo So do I. I was happy then. My heart and hands were at peace. My name called me to the throne, and I had only to let the sun rise and set to see all of human hopes flourish around me. Men had done me neither evil nor good; but I was good and to my eternal misfortune I decided I would be great. I have to confess: if Providence drove me to resolve to kill a tyrant, whoever he might be, pride drove me to it as well. What more can I tell you? All the world's Cæsars made me think of Brutus.

Filippo Pride in virtue is a noble pride. Why should you be ashamed of it?

Lorenzo Unless you go mad you will never know the kinds of thoughts that consumed me. To understand the feverish exaltation that engendered in me the Lorenzo speaking to you now, my brain and my innards would have to be laid bare with a scalpel. A statue coming down from its pedestal to walk among men might be like what I became the day I began to live with the idea that I had to be a Brutus.

Filippo You amaze me more and more.

Lorenzo First I tried to kill Pope Clement VII. I was not able to, because they banished me from Rome before the time was ripe. I began my work all over again with Alessandro. I wanted to act alone, without any man's help. I was working for humanity; but my pride remained isolated amid all my philanthropic dreams. So I had to undertake by deception a hand-to-hand struggle with my enemy. I did not want to make the masses rise up or achieve the chattering fame of a paralytic like Cicero. I wanted to get at the man himself, struggle hand-to-hand with living tyranny, kill it and after that take my bloody sword up onto the speakers' rostrum and make the smell of Alessandro's blood rise up into the orators' noses and warm their pompous brains.

Filippo What a mind of steel you have, my friend, what a mind of steel!

Lorenzo The task I had set for myself with Alessandro was a hard one. Florence was drowning in blood and wine, as it is today. The Emperor and the Pope had made a butcher-boy Duke. To please my cousin, I had to come to him borne by the tears of families. To become his friend and gain his trust I had to kiss the remnants of his orgies off his thick lips. I was as pure as a lily and yet I did not shrink from that task. Let us not speak of what I became as a result of that. You must understand what I suffered, and there are wounds from which you cannot strip off the dressing with impunity. I became a depraved, cowardly man, an object of shame and contempt. What does it matter? That is not the question.

Filippo You bow your head; your eyes are wet.

Lorenzo No, I won't blush: plaster masks cannot summon a blush to the service of shame. I did what I did. All you need know is that I have succeeded in my undertaking. Alessandro will soon go to a certain place that he will not leave on his own two feet. I have come to the end of my pains; you may be sure, Filippo, that a wild ox is not entangled by more nets or slip knots, when the drover slaughters him on the plain, than I have woven around my bastard. That heart, which even an army could not have penetrated in a year, is now laid bare under my hand. All I have to do is let my dagger fall, and it will be pierced. Everything will be done. Now do you know what is happening to me and what I want to warn you about?

Filippo You are our Brutus if you are telling the truth.

Lorenzo I believed I was a Brutus, my poor Filippo. I remembered the golden wand covered with bark. Now I know what men are like, and I advise you not to get involved.

Filippo Why not?

Lorenzo Oh, you have lived all alone, Filippo. Like a shining beacon, you have remained motionless on the shore of the sea of mankind, and you have looked at the reflection of your own light in the waters. From the depths of your solitude, you thought the ocean was magnificent, under the splendid canopy of the heavens. You did not count each wave, you did not sound its depths; you were full of confidence in God's creation. But in the meantime I did plunge; I dived into the stormy sea of life. I traveled through all its depths, protected by my glass bell. While you were admiring the surface, I saw the debris of shipwrecks, the skeletons, the Leviathans.

Filippo Your sadness breaks my heart.

Lorenzo It is because I see you the way I once was, and on the verge of doing what I did, that I am speaking this way. I do not have contempt for men; the error of books and historians is to show them different than they are. Life is like a city: you can stay there for fifty or sixty years without seeing anything but boulevards and palaces. But you had better not go into the taverns or linger, on your way home, by windows in the slum neighborhoods. Here is my advice, Filippo: if it is a question of saving your children, I suggest you keep still; that is the best way to have them sent back to you with a little warning. If it is a question of attempting something for mankind, I advise you to cut off your arms, because it won't take long for you to notice that nobody but you has any.

Filippo I can understand that the role you are playing has given you such ideas. If I understand you, you have followed a horrid path toward a sublime goal, and you believe that everything is like what you have seen.

Lorenzo I have awakened from my dreams, nothing more. I am telling you of the danger of having them. I know what life is like, and it is a nasty business, believe me. Don't stick your hand into it if you have any respect left.

Filippo Stop. Do not break the staff of my old age like a reed. I believe in everything that you call dreams: I believe in virtue, modesty, and freedom.

Lorenzo And am I not here in the gutter, "Lorenzaccio"? And the children don't throw muck at me? Their daughters' beds are still warm with my sweat, and yet fathers don't take up their knives and their brooms to strike me dead as I walk by! Inside the ten thousand houses you see there, the seventh generation will still speak of the night I entered; and not one of them spews forth an ax-head at the sight of me, to cleave me in two like a rotten log? I breathe the air you breathe, Filippo. My striped silk cloak drags lazily over the fine sand of the footpaths. Not a single drop of poison falls into my morning chocolate... What am I saying? Oh, Filippo, penniless mothers shamefully lift up their daughters' veils when I stop at their doorsteps. They show me their beauty with a smile more vile than Judas's kiss, while I, pinching the girl's chin, clench my fists in rage as I jingle four or five measly gold pieces in my pocket.

Filippo The tempter should not despise the weak. Why tempt them, if you are in doubt?

Lorenzo Am I a Satan? God in heaven, I can still remember it! I would have wept with the first girl I seduced if she had not burst out laughing. When I began to play my role as the modern Brutus, I walked in my new clothes, of the great brotherhood of vice, like a ten-year-old child wearing the giant of the fable's armor. I thought that corruption was a sign, and that only monsters bore it on their brows. I had begun to say aloud that my twenty years of virtue were a stifling mask. Oh, Filippo, then I plunged into life and I saw that at my approach everyone was doing just as I did. All the masks fell before my gaze. Mankind lifted its robe and showed me its monstrous nakedness as if I were a worthy adept. I saw men as they were, and I said to myself: Who am I working for, then? As I walked through the streets of Florence with my ghost by my side I would gaze about me, I would look for faces that heartened me, and I would ask myself: "When I have struck my blow, will that one profit from it?" I saw the proponents of a republic in their studies; I went into shops, I listened and I watched. I recorded the words of the people, I saw the effect that tyranny exercised over them; during patriotic banquets[50] I drank the wine that breeds rhetoric and metaphors. I drank in the most virtuous tears, between two kisses. I waited and waited for mankind to show me something decent on its face. I watched as a lover watches his betrothed, waiting for the wedding day.

Filippo If you saw nothing but evil I pity you but I cannot believe you. Evil exists, but not without good, as darkness exists, but not without light.

Lorenzo You wish to see in me only a despiser of men; that is insulting to me. I know perfectly well that there are good men. But what use are they? What do they do? In what way do they act? What difference does it make that the conscience is alive if the arm is dead? There are certain angles from which everything becomes good: a dog is a faithful friend; you can find in him the best of servants, just as you can see that he wallows in corpses and the tongue he licks his master with smells of carrion a mile away. All I can see is that I am doomed, and men will no more profit from it than they will understand me.

Filippo My poor child, you are breaking my heart! But if you are a decent man, you will become so again once you have freed your country. It rejoices my old heart to think that you are a decent man, Lorenzo. So you will throw off the hideous disguise that disfigures you and you will once again be made of a metal as pure as the bronze statues of Harmodius and Aristogiton.[51]

Lorenzo Filippo, Filippo, I once was a decent man. The hand that once has lifted the veil of truth can no longer let it drop again. It remains motionless until death, still holding that terrible veil, and raising it higher and higher over men's heads until the angel of eternal sleep stops his eyes.

Filippo All illnesses can be cured. Vice is an illness, too.

Lorenzo It is too late. I have become accustomed to this life. Vice once was a garment to me; now it is glued to my skin. I really am a panderer, and when I joke about people like me, I feel deadly serious in the midst of my amusement. Brutus[52] played the fool to kill Tarquin; what astounds me is that he did not lose his mind in the process. Follow my example, Filippo, that is all I can say to you: do not work for the good of your country.

Filippo If I were to believe you, it seems to me the sky would become forever dark and in my old age I would be condemned to feel my way along. It is quite possible that you have taken a dangerous route; why should I not take another one that would lead to the same point? My intention is to appeal to the people and to act openly.

Lorenzo Beware, Filippo; the man who is telling you knows why he is saying it. Take whatever path you want but you will still be dealing with men.

Filippo I believe in the decency of those who call for a republic.

Lorenzo I shall make a bet with you. I am going to kill Alessandro. Once my blow is struck, if the republicans do what they should, it will be easy to for them establish a republic, the most beautiful one that ever flourished on the earth. If they have the people on their side, it is as good as done. I wager with you that neither they nor the people will do a thing. All I ask of you is not to get involved in it. Speak, if you want, but mind your words and even more your actions. Let me strike my blow; your hands are pure and I have nothing to lose.

Filippo Do it and you will see.

Lorenzo So be it—but remember this. Do you see the family around the table in that little house? Don't they look like human beings? They have a body, and a soul in that body. And yet, if I felt like going into their house all by myself as you see me here and stabbing their eldest son in the midst of them, there would not be a single knife raised against me.

Filippo You horrify me. How can the heart remain noble when one has hands like yours?

Lorenzo Come now, let us go back to your palace and try to get your children freed.

Filippo But why are you going to kill the Duke if you have such ideas?

Lorenzo Why? You are asking me?

Filippo If you think that his murder will do no good for your country, how can you commit it?

Lorenzo You ask me to my face? Just look at me: I once was fair, at peace and virtuous.

Filippo I feel as if you were opening up an abyss before me!

Lorenzo You ask me why I am killing Alessandro? Do you want me to take poison or jump in the Arno? Do you want me to turn into a ghost, and when I strike this skeleton *(he beats his chest)* no sound to be heard? If I am just a shadow of myself, do you want me to cut off the only thread that binds my heart today to a few fibers of my former heart? Do you realize that this murder is all that I have left of my virtue? Do you realize that for two years I have been slipping down a steep wall, and this murder is the only blade of grass that I have been able to clutch at with my fingernails? Do you think I have no more pride because I have no more shame? Would you like me to let the enigma of my life die in silence? Yes, it is quite sure, if I could return to virtue, if my apprenticeship in vice could melt away, perhaps I would spare that ox-drover. But I like wine, gambling and women, do you understand? If you speaking with me here respect anything in me, it is my murder you respect, perhaps precisely because you would not commit it. The advocates of the republic have been showering mud and infamy on me for long enough, you see; my ears have been ringing and men's execration has been poisoning the bread I chew for long enough. I am sick of seeing myself despised by arrant cowards who assail me with insults so as to be excused from killing me as they ought. I am sick of hearing men's prattle squalling in the wind. Humankind must get some hint of who I am and what it is. Thank God, perhaps I shall kill Alessandro tomorrow; in a couple of days it will be over. Those who circle about me, goggling at me as if I were some monstrous curiosity brought back from the New World, will be able to clear their throats and empty their windbags all they want. Whether men understand me or not, whether they take action or not, I shall have said all I have to say. I shall get them to sharpen their writing-quills even if I do not get them to clean off their pikes, and mankind will bear my sword's mark on its cheek in streaks of blood. Whatever they want to call me, Brutus or Herostratus,[53] I would not like them to forget me. My whole life hangs from the point of my dagger; whether or not Providence looks around when it hears me strike, I am playing heads or tails with human nature on Alessandro's grave. In two days, mankind appears before the tribunal of my will.

Filippo All this amazes me and in all you say there are things that grieve me and others that delight me. But Piero and Tommaso are in jail and I cannot trust anyone but myself in this matter. My anger struggles in vain to hold itself in check; my vitals are too keenly moved. You may be right but I must take action. I am going to assemble my relations.

Lorenzo As you will; but beware. Keep my secret, even from your friends, that is all I ask of you. *(Exeunt.)*

Scene 4.

The Soderini palace.

(Enter Caterina, reading a letter.)

Caterina "Lorenzo must have spoken to you of me; but who could speak worthily to you of a love like mine? Let my pen tell you what my lips cannot say, and what my heart would like to sign with its blood.

Alessandro de' Medici"

If my name were not on the address, I would think that the messenger had made a mistake. What I have read makes me doubt my eyes. *(Enter Maria.)* Oh, my dear mother, see what has been written to me! Unravel this mystery for me if you can.

Maria You unfortunate woman! He is in love with you! Where has he seen you? Where have you spoken to him?

Caterina Nowhere. A messenger brought this to me as I was coming out of church.

Maria He says that Lorenzo must have spoken of him to you? Oh, Caterina, to have a son like him! Yes, to make his mother's sister the Duke's mistress—not even his mistress, oh, my daughter! What do they call such creatures? I cannot say it. Yes, that was all that Lorenzo lacked. Come with me, I want to show him this letter already opened, and see before God how he will reply.

Caterina I thought the Duke was in love... Pardon me, mother, but I thought that the Duke loved Countess Cibo; they had told me...

Maria That is right, he did love her, if he is capable of that.

Caterina He no longer loves her? Oh, how can anyone offer such a heart without feeling shame? Come, mother, come along to Lorenzo's room.

Maria Give me your arm. I do not know what I have been feeling for the past few days. I have had a fever every night. It is true that it has not left me for the past three months. I have suffered too much, my poor Caterina; why did you read me that letter? I cannot bear anything any more. I am no longer young, and yet it seems to me I could grow young again under certain conditions. But everything I see draws me toward the grave. Come along, let me lean on you, my poor child. I shall not give you that trouble for very long. *(Exeunt.)*

Scene 5.

The Marquise Cibo's room.

Marquise *(in her finery, before a mirror)* When I think that it has happened, it seems to me like some news I might suddenly learn. What a precipice life is! Why, it is already nine o'clock and it is the Duke I am expecting in this gown! Come what may, I am going to try out my power. *(Enter the Cardinal.)*

Cardinal What finery, Marquise. Those flowers have a heavenly scent.

Marquise I cannot see you now, Cardinal. I am expecting a woman friend; you must excuse me.

Cardinal I shall leave you, I shall leave you. That boudoir whose half-open door I see over there is a little paradise. Shall I go and wait there for you?

Marquise I am in a hurry, excuse me. Not in my boudoir; wherever you wish.

Cardinal I shall come back at a more favorable time. *(Exit.)*

Marquise Why does that priest always show up? Why does that bald-headed vulture keep circling around me, so that I always find him behind my back when I turn around? Can it be that the hour of my death is near? *(Enter a page who whispers in her ear.)* Yes, yes, I am going. Oh, you cannot get used to being treated like a servant, poor vain heart. *(Exit.)*

Scene 6.

The Marquise's boudoir.

(The Marquise, the Duke.)

Marquise That is my way of thinking. I would love you like that.

Duke Words, words, nothing more.

Marquise It is so little for you men! To sacrifice the tranquillity of one's life, the holy virtue of honor, sometimes even one's children! To live for one sole being in the world! To "give oneself," since after all that is what it is called! But it is not worth the bother: why listen to a woman? A woman who speaks of other things than dresses and wantonness is unheard of.

Duke You are dreaming with your eyes wide open.

Marquise Yes, by heaven! Yes, I had a dream! Alas, only kings never do: all the fantasies of their whims are transformed into realities and even their nightmares are turned into marble. Alessandro! Alexander! What a name that is: "I can if I will!" Oh, God Himself knows nothing greater: hearing that name, the people's hands come together in fearful prayer and the pale flock of men holds its breath to listen.

Duke Let us not speak of that any more, my dear, it is so tiresome.

Marquise Do you know what it means to be a king? To have a hundred thousand hands at the end of one's arms! To be the ray of sunlight that dries men's tears! To be fortune and misfortune! Oh, what a deadly shiver that can give! How that old man in the Vatican would tremble if you spread your wings, my eagle! The Emperor is so far away! The garrison is so devoted to you. Besides, you may slaughter an army but you cannot slaughter a people. The day you have the entire nation on your side, when you are at the head of a free body, when you say: As the Doge of Venice weds the Adriatic, thus I place my golden ring on the finger of my beautiful Florence and her children are my children... Oh, do you know what a people that takes its benefactor into its arms is like? Do you know what it means to be borne like a cherished suckling child on the vast ocean of men? Do you know what it means to be pointed out by a father to his child?

Duke What I care about is taxes: as long as they are paid, what else matters to me?

Marquise But don't you see, they will assassinate you.—The cobblestones will come forth from the ground and crush you. Oh, posterity! Have you never seen that phantom at your bedside? Have you never wondered what those who are in the wombs of the living will think of you? And you are still alive, there is still time! You have but to say a word. Do you remember the father of our country? Come now, it is easy to be great when one is king. Declare Florence independent; call for fulfillment of the treaty with the Emperor; draw your sword and show it. They will tell you to put it back in its sheath, because its glint hurts their eyes. Just think how young you are! Nothing has been decided on your account yet.—There is broad indulgence for princes in the hearts of the people, and the public's gratitude is a deep river of forgetfulness for their past errors. You have been badly advised, you have been deceived.—But there is still time; you have but to speak; while you are still living, the page in God's book has not yet been turned.

Duke Enough, my dear, enough.

Marquise Oh, when it *is* turned! When a wretched gardener paid by the day comes and reluctantly waters a few shabby daisies around Alessandro's grave—when the poor joyously breathe the free air and no longer see the dark meteor of your power hovering over them; when they shake their heads as they speak of you; when they count their families' graves around your own, are you sure you will sleep peacefully in your final sleep? —You never go to church and you are concerned only about taxes, but are you sure eternity is deaf and there are no echoes of life in the ghastly realm of the dead? Do you know where the tears of the people go when the wind bears them off?

Duke What a pretty leg this is![54]

Marquise Listen to me. You are flighty, I know; but you are not malicious. No, by God, you are not, you cannot be. Come now, force yourself—reflect a moment, just a moment, on what I am saying. Is there nothing in all of that? Am I really a madwoman?

Duke All that does go through my mind; but what am I doing that is so wrong? I am as good as my fellow rulers; in truth I am better than the Pope. You remind me of the Strozzi with your speeches—and you know I detest them. You want me to revolt against the Emperor: the Emperor is my father-in-law, my dearest. You imagine that the Florentines do not love me; well, I am sure that they do. Ha, damn it, even if you were right, who do you want me to be afraid of?

Marquise You are not afraid of your people but you are afraid of the Emperor. You have killed or dishonored hundreds of citizens, and you think you have done enough if you wear a coat of mail under your shirt.

Duke Peace! None of that.

Marquise Oh, I am letting myself get carried away! I am saying things I do not mean. My dear, who does not know that you are brave? You are brave, as you are handsome; the evil that you do is owing to your youth, to your mind—what shall I say, it is the blood coursing violently through your fiery veins, it is the stifling heat weighing down on us.—I beg you, let me not have sacrificed myself totally; let my name, my poor love for you, not be written down on some odious list. I am a woman, it is true, and if beauty is everything for women, many others are worth more than I am. But, tell me, have you nothing, absolutely nothing here! *(She strikes his breast.)*

Duke What a devil! Come sit over here, my little darling.

Marquise Well, yes, I will admit it, I do have some ambition: not for me but for you! For you and my beloved Florence! Oh, God knows how much I am suffering.

Duke You are suffering? What is the matter?

Marquise No, I am not suffering. Listen! Listen! I can see that you are bored with me. You count the minutes, you look away; don't go away yet, this is perhaps the last time I shall see you. Listen! I tell you that Florence calls you its latest plague, and there is not a cottage in which your portrait is not stuck to the walls with a knife through the heart. What does it matter if I am mad, if you hate me tomorrow? You have to know that.

Duke Woe betide you if you trifle with my anger!

Marquise Yes, woe betide me! Woe betide me!

Duke Some other time—tomorrow morning, if you wish—we can see each other again and talk about that. Do not be angry if I leave you right now: I have to go hunting.

Marquise Yes, woe betide me! Woe betide me!

Duke What is the matter? You look as somber as hell itself. Why the devil have you ever gotten mixed up in politics? Come, come, your little role as a woman, and a real woman, suits you so well. You are too religious; you will get over that. Come help me put my clothes back on; I am all mussed up.

Marquise Farewell, Alessandro. *(The Duke kisses her.—Enter Cardinal Cibo.)*

Cardinal Oh!—Excuse me, your Highness, I thought my sister was alone. I am so clumsy, the blame should be all on me. I beg you to forgive me.

Duke What do you mean? Come, now, Malaspina, that reeks of the priest. Are you supposed to see things like that? Come, now: what the devil does this matter to you? *(Exeunt together.)*

Marquise *(alone, holding her husband's portrait)* Where are you now, Lorenzo? It is past noon; you are walking along the terrace near the great chestnut trees. The fat heifers are grazing around you; your farm hands are dining in the shade; the lawn lifts up its whitish cloak in the sun's rays; the trees, tended by your care, murmur reverently over the white head of their old master while the echo of our long archways dutifully repeats the sound of your tranquil steps. Oh, my Lorenzo, I have wasted the treasure of your honor! I have doomed your final years to ridicule and doubt. You will no longer press a heart worthy of your own against your breast. A trembling hand will bring you your evening meal when you return from the hunt.

Scene 7.

The Strozzi's.

(The forty Strozzi at the supper table.)

Filippo Let us sit down to supper, my children.

Guests Why are there two empty seats?

Filippo Piero and Tommaso are in jail.

Guests Why?

Filippo Because Salviati insulted my daughter, sitting here, at the Monteoliveto fair, in public and in the presence of her brother, Leone. Piero and Tommaso killed Salviati, and Alessandro de' Medici had them arrested to avenge his procurer's death.

Guests Death to the Medici!

Filippo I have gathered my family together to tell it of my troubles and ask for help. Let us have supper and then go forth, sword in hand, to demand the return of my two sons, if you have enough courage.

Guests We will do as you say.

Filippo It is time for all that to end, don't you see? They would kill our sons and dishonor our daughters. It is time for Florence to teach these bastards what the right to life and death means. The Council of Eight has no right to condemn my children and as for me, I would not survive them, you see.

Guests Have no fear, Filippo, we are with you.

Filippo I am the head of the family. How could I allow myself to be insulted? We are as great as the Medici; so are the Rucellai, the Aldobrandini and twenty others. Why should they be able to cut our children's throats rather than we theirs? If we were to light a powder keg in the vaults of the citadel, the German garrison would be routed. What would be left to the Medici? That is where their power lies; apart from that they are nothing. Are we men or not? Will we allow them to strike down the families of Florence with the blow of an ax, and to tear from our native soil roots as old as she is? They are starting with us, so it is up to us to stand firm. Our first cry of alarm, like a falconer's shrill whistle, will summon an entire army of eagles driven out from their nest back to Florence. They are not far away. They are circling around the city, gazing at its bell-towers. We shall fly the black flag of plague, and they will come running at that signal of death. Those are the colors of divine wrath. This evening, let us first go free our sons; tomorrow we shall march together with drawn swords to the doors of all the great families. There are eighty palaces in Florence, and from each of them, when freedom knocks, will issue forth a troop equal to our own.

Guests Long live freedom!

Filippo I call God to witness that it is violence that forces me to draw my sword. I have remained a good, peaceful citizen for sixty years. I have never harmed a soul in all the world. Half of my fortune has been used to succor the unfortunate.

Guests That is true.

Filippo It is a just revenge that drives me to revolt; I have rebelled because God made me a father. I am not driven by any impulse of ambition or of self-interest or pride. My cause is just, honorable and holy. Fill your cups and stand up. Our revenge is a holy wafer that we can break without fear and partake of in the eyes of God. I drink to the Medici's death!

Guests *(standing up and drinking)* To the Medici's death!

Luisa *(setting her glass down)* Oh, I am dying.

Filippo What is the matter, daughter, my beloved child? What is the matter? My God, what has happened to you? My God, my God, how pale you are! Speak, what is the matter? Tell your father. Help! Help! A doctor! Quickly, there is no time to waste.

Luisa I am going to die, I am going to die. *(She dies.)*

Filippo She is going, my friends, she is going! A doctor! My daughter has been poisoned! *(He falls to his knees next to Luisa.)*

A guest Cut her corset open. Make her drink warm water. If it is poison, she must have warm water. *(Servants come running.)*

Other gu. Slap her hands. Open the windows and slap her hands.

Other gu. Perhaps it is only a fainting spell. She may have drunk too quickly.

Other gu. The poor child! How calm her expression is! She cannot have died so suddenly.

Filippo My child! Are you dead, Luisa, my beloved child?

First gu. Here comes the doctor. *(Enter a doctor.)*

Second gu. Hurry, hurry; tell us if it is poison.

Filippo She has just fainted, hasn't she?

Doctor The poor girl! She is dead. *(Deep silence reigns through the hall; Filippo is still kneeling next to Luisa, holding her hands.)*

A guest It is the Medici's poison. We must not leave Filippo in the state he is in. His stillness is frightening.

Other gu. I am sure I am not mistaken. There was a servant at the table who worked for Salviati's wife.

Other gu. He must have done it, there is not doubt. Let us go out and get him. *(Exeunt.)*

First gu. Filippo refuses to answer anything said to him. He has been struck by lightning.

Other gu. This is terrible! This murder is outrageous!

Other gu. It cries out to heaven for revenge. Let us go out and slit Alessandro's throat.

Other gu. Yes, let us go out. Death to Alessandro! He is the one who ordered all this. What fools we are! His hatred for us was not born yesterday. We are acting too late.

Other gu. Salviati was not after Luisa for himself: he was working for the Duke. Come, let us go out, even if they were to kill us all, to the last man.

Filippo My friends, you will bury my daughter, won't you? *(He puts on his cloak.)* In the garden, behind the fig-trees. Farewell, good friends, farewell, God be with you.

A guest Where are you going, Filippo?

Filippo I have had enough, don't you see? I have had as much as I can bear. I have two sons in jail and now my daughter is dead. I have had enough, I am going away.

A guest You are going away without taking revenge?

Filippo Yes, yes. Just place my daughter in her shroud, but do not bury her. I am the one who must bury her. I shall do it in my own way, at a monastery I know; some monks will come and get her tomorrow. What good does it do to look at her? She is dead, so it is useless. Farewell, my friends, go back home; God be with you.

A guest Do not let him go out, he has lost his senses.

Other gu. It is horrible! I feel ready to faint in this hall. *(Exit.)*

Filippo Do not restrain me. Do not shut me up in a room with my daughter's body. Let me leave.

A guest Avenge yourself, Filippo; let us avenge you. Your Luisa will be our Lucretia![55] We shall make Alessandro drink the rest of her glass.

Other gu. Another Lucretia! We are going to swear on her body to die for our country! Go home, Filippo, think of your country. Do not go back on your word.

Filippo Freedom, revenge, don't you see, that is all very fine. Two of my sons are in jail and now my daughter is dead. If I stay here everything will die around me. The important thing is for me to leave and for you to be quiet. When my door and my windows are shut, no one will think of the Strozzi any longer. If they remain open, I shall see you all fall dead, one after the other. I am old, don't you see? It is time for me to close up shop. Farewell, friends, be quiet; if I am not here, no one will harm you. I am going off to Venice straight away.

A guest There is a terrible storm. Stay here tonight.

Filippo Do not bury the poor child. My old monks will come tomorrow and take her away. God of justice, God of justice, what have I ever done to you? *(He runs off.)*

ACT FOUR
Scene 1.

The Duke's palace.

(Enter the Duke and Lorenzo.)

Duke I wish I had been there. There must have been more than one face flushed with rage. But I can't begin to guess who might have poisoned that Luisa.

Lorenzo I can't, either; unless it was you.

Duke Filippo must be furious! I have heard he has left for Venice. Thank God, that way I am delivered from the unbearable old fogy. As for his dear family, it will be so kind as to keep still. Do you know, they almost fomented a little rebellion in their neighborhood? Two of my Germans were killed.

Lorenzo What bothers me most is that that fine fellow Salviati has lost a leg. Have you found your coat of mail?

Duke No, to tell the truth. I am more annoyed than I can say.

Lorenzo Watch out for Giomo; he is the one who stole it. What are you wearing in its place?

Duke Nothing; I cannot stand any other one; there are none as light as it was.

Lorenzo That is too bad for you.

Duke You haven't spoken to me about your aunt.

Lorenzo It is just an oversight, for she adores you. She hasn't been able to rest since the star of your love began to shine in her poor heart. For mercy's sake, my lord, have pity on her. Say when you are willing to receive her and at what time she will be allowed to sacrifice what little virtue she has to you.

Duke Are you serious?

Lorenzo Deadly serious. I would just like to see an aunt of mine not sleep with you.

Duke Where may I see her?

Lorenzo In my bedroom, my lord. I shall have some white curtains hung around my bed and a pot of mignonette placed on my table. After that I shall write down on your daybook that my aunt will be in her nightgown at precisely midnight so that you don't forget after supper.

Duke I don't think I will. Plague take it, Caterina is a piece fit for a king. Eh, tell me, you clever boy, are you really sure that she will come? How did you manage it?

Lorenzo I shall tell you all about it.

Duke I am going to look at a horse I just bought; farewell, I shall see you this evening. Come and get me after supper and we shall go together to your house. As for the Cibo woman, I am fed up with her. Just yesterday I had to put up with her during the entire hunt. Good evening, darling. *(Exit.)*

Lorenzo *(alone)* So it is all set. This evening I shall take him to my house and tomorrow the partisans of a republic will know what they have to do, for the Duke of Florence will be dead. I have to let Scoronconcolo know. Fly quickly, sun, if you are anxious to hear the news this night will tell you tomorrow. *(Exit.)*

Scene 2.

A street.

(Piero and Tommaso Strozzi, coming from prison.)

Piero I was sure that the Council of Eight would send me home absolved and you, too. Come on, let us knock on our door and go embrace our father. That is strange, the shutters are closed!

Porter *(opening the door)* Alas, my lords, you have heard the news.

Piero What news? You look like a ghost that has just come from the grave, at the door of this deserted palace.

Porter Is it possible that you have not heard? *(Two monks arrive.)*

Tommaso What could we have heard? We just go out of prison. Tell us, what has happened?

Porter Alas, my poor lords, it is terrible to say!

Monks *(coming up)* Is this the Strozzi palace?

Porter Yes. What do you want?

Monks We have come to get the body of Luisa Strozzi. Here is Filippo's authorization for you to let us take it.

Piero What are you saying? Whose body did you ask for?

Monks Don't stay here, my son, you bear Filippo's resemblance on your face. There is nothing good for you to learn here.

Tommaso What? She is dead? Dead? Oh, God in heaven! *(He sits down a little way off.)*

Piero I am stronger than you think. Who killed my sister? No one dies at her age in the space of a single night without some unnatural cause. Who killed her, so I can kill him? Answer me or you are a dead man yourself.

Porter Alas! Who can say? No one knows a thing.

Piero Where is my father? Come on, Tommaso, no tears. By heaven, my heart is getting as hard as if it were going to turn to stone inside me and remain a rock for all eternity.

Monks If you are Filippo's son, come with us; we shall take you to him. He has been at our monastery since yesterday.

Piero And I won't find out who killed my sister? Listen to me, priests: if you are in God's image, you can be given an oath. By all the instruments of torture under the heavens, by all the torments of hell... No, I won't say a word. Let's go quickly, I want to see my father. Oh, God! Make what I suspect be the truth so I can crush them under my feet like grains of sand. Come on, come on, before I lose strength; don't say a word to me. This is a matter of a revenge, you see, such as divine wrath never dreamt of. *(Exeunt.)*

Scene 3.

A street.

(Lorenzo, Scoronconcolo.)

Lorenzo Go back home and come at midnight without fail. Shut yourself up in my study until someone comes and tells you.

Scoronc. Yes, my lord. *(Exit.)*

Lorenzo *(alone)* What sort of tiger did my mother dream of when she was expecting me? When I think I loved flowers, meadows and the sonnets of Petrarch, the ghost of my youth rises shivering before me. Oh, God, why do the mere words "Till tonight" make this burning joy pierce my very bones like a red-hot blade? What savage womb, what brutish couplings begot me?

Has that man done anything to me? When I place my hand here on my heart and reflect—who, hearing me say tomorrow, "I killed him," would not reply, "Why did you kill him"? It is strange. He has wronged others but he has been good to me, at least in his own way. If I had remained in peace, in the depths of my solitude at Cafaggiuolo, he would never have come to find me there, whereas I came to find him in Florence. Why? Did the ghost of my father lead me, like Orestes, toward another Ægisthus? Had he offended me then? It is strange, and yet I have abandoned everything for this action. The mere thought of this murder made my life's dreams fall to dust. I have been nothing but a ruin ever since this murder alighted in my path, like some sinister raven, and called out to me. What does that mean? A moment ago as I walked through the square I heard two men talking of a comet. Are these really the beats of a human heart I feel here under my breast bone? Oh, why has this idea kept coming back to me these past days? Am I the arm of God? Is there a cloud above my head? When I go into that room and try to pull my sword from its sheath, I am afraid I shall draw the archangel's flaming sword and fall in ashes on my prey. *(Exit.)*

Scene 4.

The Marquise Cibo's apartment.
(Enter the Cardinal and the Marquise.)

Marquise As you wish, Malaspina.

Cardinal Yes, as I wish. You had better think twice, Marquise, before trifling with me. Are you a woman like all the others? Do I have to have a golden chain around my neck and credentials in my hand for you to understand who I am? Are you waiting for a valet to shout at the top of his lungs while opening a door before me to know what my power is? Let me tell you: it is not official titles that make the man. I am neither the Pope's envoy nor Charles the Fifth's captain; I am more than that.

Marquise Yes, I know. The Emperor has sold his shadow to the devil and it walks around, decked out in a crimson robe, under the name of Cibo.

Cardinal You are Alessandro's mistress, do not forget it. And your secret is in my hands.

Marquise Do as you please with it. We shall see what use a confessor can put his conscience to.

Cardinal You are mistaken. I did not learn it from your confession. I have seen it with my own eyes: I saw you kissing the Duke. Even if you had admitted it to me in the confessional, I could still speak of it without sin since I have seen it outside of the confessional.

Marquise And so?

Cardinal Why did the Duke leave you with such a carefree step, heaving a sigh like a schoolboy when the bell rings? You sated him with that patriotism of yours, which gets mingled with all the dishes at your table like some insipid brew. What books have you read, and what kind of stupid biddy served as your governess, for you not to know that a king's mistress usually talks of other things than patriotism?

Marquise I admit that I was never clearly taught what a king's mistress is supposed to talk about. I neglected to find out more on that point, just as I also neglected to eat rice powder to fatten myself up as Turkish women do.

Cardinal It does not take much learning to keep a lover a little more than three days.

Marquise It would have been quite simple for a priest to teach such things to a woman; why didn't you advise me?

Cardinal Do you want my advice? Take your cloak and go slip into the Duke's bed. If he is expecting speeches when he sees you, prove to him that you know how not to make them at all times. Act like a sleepwalker and make sure that, if he falls asleep on your freedom-loving breast, it is not from boredom. Are you a maiden? Is there no more Cyprus wine? Don't you have some joyous song in the depths of your memory? Haven't you read Aretino?

Marquise My Lord! I have heard horrible old women whispering things like that as they shiver at the New Market. If you are not a priest, are you at least a man? Are you sure the heavens are empty, to make your very crimson blush like that?

Cardinal There is nothing so virtuous as the ear of a depraved woman. Pretend you understand me or you don't, but remember that my brother is your husband.

Marquise I can only vaguely comprehend what interest you have in tormenting me thus. You appall me: what is it you want from me?

Cardinal There are some secrets a woman must not know but that she can further by knowing their elements.

Marquise What mysterious thread of your dark thoughts would you like me to hang on to? If your desires are as frightening as your threats, speak up: at least show me the hair holding the sword up over my head.

Cardinal I can speak only in covert terms since I am not sure I can trust you. Suffice it for you to know that if you had been some other woman, you would be queen by the present time. Since you call me Cæsar's shadow, you may have noticed that it is long enough to cut off Florence's sun. Do you know how far a woman's smile can lead? Do you know how far fortunes that have their roots in the bedroom may go? Alessandro is the Pope's son, you ought to know; and when the Pope was in Bologna... But I am allowing myself to be drawn out too far.

Marquise Beware you don't make a confession in your turn. You may be my husband's brother but I am Alessandro's mistress.

Cardinal You have been, Marquise, and many others, too.

Marquise Yes, I have been, thank God, I have been.

Cardinal I was sure you would begin with your dreams. Some day, however, you will have to get to mine. Listen to me, this is not the time to be quarreling; but, in truth, you take everything seriously. Get back in Alessandro's good graces and since I hurt your feelings a moment ago when I told you how, I have no reason to repeat it now. Let yourself be led; in a year or two you will thank me. I have worked a long time to become what I am and I know how far one can go. If I were sure of you, I would tell you things that God himself will never know.

Marquise Don't raise your hopes; you may be assured of my contempt. *(She goes toward the door.)*

Cardinal Just a moment! Not so fast! Don't you hear the sound of a horse? Isn't my brother supposed to come back today or tomorrow? Do you know me for a man who does not keep his word? Go to the palace tonight or you are doomed.

Marquise In the last analysis, I can understand your being ambitious and that any means is acceptable to you. But will you speak more clearly? Come now, Malaspina, I hope I have not been corrupted absolutely for naught. If you can convince me, do so—tell me frankly, what is your aim?

Cardinal You hope you can be convinced, is that it? Do you take me for a child? Do you think you just have to rub my lips with honey to pry them open? First you must act, then I shall talk. The day you have gained the necessary power as a woman, not over the mind of Alessandro, the Duke of Florence, but over the heart of Alessandro, your lover, I shall tell you the rest and you will know what I expect.

Marquise And so, when I have read Aretino to gain initial experience, I shall have to read the secret book of your thoughts to acquire some more. Do you want me to tell you what you don't dare tell me? You are serving the Pope until the Emperor finds that you are a better servant than the Pope himself. You hope that one day the Emperor will quite really, quite completely owe Italy's enslavement to you and on that day—oh, on that day, is it not true that he who is king of half the world might well reward you with the paltry inheritance of heaven. To govern Florence by governing the Duke, you would just as soon turn yourself into a woman, if you could. When poor Ricciarda Cibo has made Alessandro carry out two or three coups, people will soon add that Ricciarda Cibo leads the Duke by the nose but that she is led by her brother-in-law. And as you say, who knows how far the people's tears, when they become an ocean, might launch your ship? Is that about it? My imagination probably cannot go as far as yours but I think that is about it.

Cardinal Go to the Duke's tonight or you are doomed.

Marquise Doomed? In what way?

Cardinal Your husband will know everything.

Marquise Go ahead, do it. I shall kill myself.

Cardinal A woman's threat! Listen here and do not toy with me. Whether you have understood me or not, go to the Duke's tonight.

Marquise No.

Cardinal Here comes your husband entering the courtyard. By all that is most holy in this world, I shall tell him everything if you say no one more time.

Marquise No, no, no! *(Enter the Marquis.)* Lorenzo, while you were at Massa, I gave myself to Alessandro; I gave myself to him, knowing who he was and what a tawdry role I was going to play. But here is a priest who wants me to play a baser one yet. He is suggesting infamous things to guarantee me the title of the Duke's mistress and to turn it to his own profit. *(She falls to her knees.)*

Marquis Are you mad? What does she mean, Malaspina?—Well, you just stand there like a statue. Is this play-acting, Cardinal? Now, then: what must I make of this?

Cardinal Ah, by the body of Jesus Christ! *(Exit.)*

Marquis She has fainted. Ho, there! Someone bring some vinegar.

Scene 5.

Lorenzo's bedroom.

(Lorenzo, two servants.)

Lorenzo When you have put those flowers on the table and these at the foot of the bed, light a good fire, but in such a way that the flame will not blaze tonight and the coals provide heat but not light. Give me the key and go to bed. *(Enter Caterina.)*

Caterina Our mother is ill. Won't you come and see her, Renzo?

Lorenzo My mother is ill?

Caterina Alas, I cannot hide the truth from you. I received a letter yesterday from the Duke and he wrote in it that you must have told me of his love for me. Reading that did a great deal of harm to Maria.

Lorenzo And yet I had not spoken to you of it. Did you not tell her that I had nothing to do with it?

Caterina I did. Why is your room so beautiful tonight and so neat? I didn't think that neatness was your strong point.

Lorenzo So the Duke wrote to you? It is strange I didn't know. And tell me, what do you make of his letter?

Caterina What do I make of it?

Lorenzo Yes, Alessandro's proposal. What does that innocent little heart make of it?

Caterina What do you want me to make of it?

Lorenzo Weren't you flattered? So many women covet that love! It would be such a fine title to achieve, being the mistress of... Go away, Caterina, go tell my mother that I am coming right away. Leave this room. Leave me alone! *(Exit Caterina.)* By the heavens! What a man of wax I must be! Has vice, like Deianira's robe,[56] become so deep rooted in my fibers that I cannot control my tongue and the air coming forth from my lips becomes a panderer in spite of myself? I was ready to pervert Caterina. I think I would pervert my mother if I took it into my mind. For God knows what kind of cord and bow the gods have drawn in my head and how powerful are the arrows they shoot. If all men are sparks from a gigantic hearth, assuredly the unknown being who modeled me dropped a firebrand instead of a spark into this feeble, trembling body. I can deliberate and choose, but not retrace my steps once I have decided. Oh, God, do not young men of fashion glory in their vice and do young boys have anything more urgent than to hasten to debauchery when they leave school? What a quagmire the human race must be to rush into taverns this way, with its lips hungry for depravity, while I, who only wanted to put on a mask resembling their face and who went to brothels with the unshakable resolution to remain pure under my soiled clothing, can neither find my former self nor wash my hands, even in blood! Poor Caterina! You would die, though, like Luisa Strozzi, or you would let yourself fall into the eternal abyss if I were not here. Oh, Alessandro, I am not a believer! But I would very much want you to say your prayers before you enter this room tonight. Is Caterina not virtuous, irreproachable? And yet how many words would it take to make that ignorant dove the prey of that red-maned bully-boy? When I think I almost talked! How many daughters cursed by their fathers are prowling on the street corners or looking at their shaved head in the broken mirror of a cell, who were just as good as Caterina and who listened to a less clever pimp than me! Well, I have committed many a crime; and if ever my life is weighed in the scales by some judge or other, on one side there will be a mountain of weeping but on the other there may be a drop of pure milk fallen from Caterina's breast, which will have suckled honest children. *(Exit.)*

Scene 6.

A valley, with a monastery in the background.

(Enter Filippo Strozzi and two monks. Some novices are carrying Luisa's coffin; they set it down in a grave.)

Filippo Before you put her in her final bed, let me embrace her. When she was in bed, I used to lean over her like this to give her a goodnight kiss. Her pensive eyes were half shut; but they would open again at the first rays of the sun like two sky-blue flowers. She would get up gently with a smile on her lips and she would come to return her father's evening kiss. Her heavenly face charmed what is often a sad time, the awakening of a man who is tired of life. One more day, I would think on seeing the dawn, another furrow in the field I till! But then I would see my daughter and life would appear to me in her beauty's form and the light of day would be welcome. *(The grave is covered.)*

Piero *(off stage)* This way, come over this way.

Filippo You will never arise from your bed again. You will never run barefoot across this lawn to come and meet your father again. Oh, my Luisa! God alone knew who you were, and I, I, I!

Piero *(entering)* There are a hundred men in Sestino who have just arrived from Piedmont. Come, Filippo, the time for weeping is past.

Filippo My child, do you know what the time for weeping is?

Piero The exiles have gathered in Sestino. It is time to think of revenge. Let us march boldly on Florence with our small army. If we can arrive at the right time of night and surprise the citadel's outposts, it will all be over. By heaven, I shall erect a different mausoleum to my sister than this one!

Filippo But I shall not. Go without me, my friends.

Piero We cannot do it without you; you must know that the allies are counting on your name. King Francis the First himself is waiting for you to make a move in favor of liberty. He has written to you as the head of the Florentine pro-liberty faction. Here is his letter.

Filippo *(He opens the letter.)* Tell the man who brought you this letter to give this answer to the King of France: the day that Filippo bears arms against his country, he will have gone mad.

Piero What is this new dictum?

Filippo It suits me.

Piero And so you doom the cause of the exiles for the pleasure of making a pronouncement? Think twice, father, we are not talking about a passage from Pliny. Reflect before you say no.

Filippo I have known for sixty years how to answer the King of France's letter.

Piero This is beyond me! You are going to force me to say things... Come with us, father, I beg you. When I went to the Pazzi's, did you not say to me: "Take me along"? Were things different then?

Filippo Very different. An insulted father who leaves his house sword in hand with his friends to call for justice is very different from a rebel who bears arms against his country in open country and against the law.

Piero As if it was a question of calling for justice! It was a question of killing Alessandro! What has changed today? You do not love your country, or else you would take advantage of such an opportunity.

Filippo An opportunity, good God, you call this an opportunity! *(He strikes the grave.)*

Piero Please listen to us.

Filippo My grief is not ambitious. Leave me alone, I have said enough.

Piero You stubborn old man! You relentless phrase-maker! You will be the cause of our ruin.

Filippo Be still, you arrogant boy! Get out of here!

Piero I cannot express what it is I am feeling. Go wherever you want, we shall act without you this time. Ha, by God, let it not be said that everything was lost for want of a Latin translator. *(Exit.)*

Filippo Your time is up, Filippo! All this means that your time is up. *(Exit.)*

Scene 7.

The banks of the Arno. The waterfront; a long row of palaces can be seen. (Enter Lorenzo.)

Lorenzo Now the sun is setting. I have no time to waste and yet everything here seems a waste of time. *(He knocks on a door.)* Hey, there! Signor Alamanno! Hey, there!

Alamanno (on the terrace) Who is it? What do you want of me?

Lorenzo I have come to let you know the Duke is going to be killed tonight. Take steps with your friends for tomorrow, if you love freedom.

Alamanno Who is going to kill Alessandro?

Lorenzo Lorenzo de' Medici.

Alamanno Is that you, Renzinaccio? Ha, come on in and have supper with some cheerful companions here in my drawing room.

Lorenzo I do not have time. Get ready to act tomorrow.

Alamanno So you are going to kill the Duke? Come now, you have drunk too much wine. *(Exit.)*

Lorenzo *(alone)* Perhaps it is wrong of me to say that I am the one who will kill Alessandro; people refuse to believe me. *(He knocks on another door.)* Hey, there, Signor Pazzi, hey!

Pazzi *(on his terrace)* Who called me?

Lorenzo I have come to tell you that the Duke is going to be killed tonight. Try and do something tomorrow for the freedom of Florence.

Pazzi Who is going to kill the Duke?

Lorenzo What does that matter, go ahead and do something with your friends. I cannot tell you the man's name.

Pazzi You are mad, you rascal, go to the devil. *(Exit.)*

Lorenzo *(alone)* It is clear that if I don't say it is me, they believe me even less. *(He knocks on a door.)* Hey, there, Signor Corsini!

Corsini *(on his terrace)* What is the matter?

Lorenzo Duke Alessandro is to be killed tonight.

Corsini Really, Lorenzo, if you are drunk go and play jokes somewhere else! You wounded one of my horses for no good reason at the Nasi's ball, the devil take you! *(Exit.)*

Lorenzo Poor Florence! Poor Florence! *(Exit.)*

Scene 8.

A plain.

(Enter Piero Strozzi and two exiles.)

Piero My father won't come. I tried but I could not get him to listen to reason.

First exile I won't announce that to my comrades. It would be enough to discourage them completely.

Piero Why? Get on your horses tonight and ride flat out to Sestino; I shall be there tomorrow morning. Tell them that Filippo has refused but Piero does not.

First exile The confederates require Filippo's name: we shall accomplish nothing without it.

Piero Filippo's family name is the same as mine. Say Strozzi is coming and that will suffice.

First exile They will ask me which of the Strozzi, and if I do not answer Filippo nothing will happen.

Piero You idiot! Do what you are told and just answer for yourself. How can you know in advance that nothing will happen?

First exile My lord, there is no need to mistreat people.

Piero Come now, get on your horse and go to Sestino.

First exile In faith, sir, my horse is tired. I rode twelve leagues over night. I don't feel like saddling it up right now.

Piero You are nothing but an ass. *(To the other exile.)* You go. You will do it better.

Second ex. My colleague is not mistaken as far as Filippo is concerned. It is certain that his name would help the cause a great deal.

Piero Cowards! Faint-hearted churls! What helps the cause is that your wives and children are starving to death, do you hear me? Filippo's name may fill their mouths but it won't fill their bellies. What kind of swine are you?

Second ex. It is no use talking with such a coarse man; let us go, comrade.

Piero Go to the devil, you rabble! And tell your confederates that if they want no part of me, the King of France does. Let them watch out, I may be given control over all of you!

Second ex. *(to the other one)* Come on, comrade, let us go have supper. I am exhausted, like you. *(Exeunt.)*

Scene 9.

A square; it is night.

(Enter Lorenzo.)

Lorenzo I shall tell him that it is due to her modesty, and take away the lamp. That is done all the time... A newlywed, for example, requires it of her husband to enter the bridal chamber, and Caterina is known to be very chaste. The poor girl! Who is, under the sun, if not she? What could come of all this is that my mother might die.

And so now it is done. Be patient! An hour is an hour and the clock just struck. If you insist, however! No, why? Take the torch out, if you want. The first time a woman surrenders that is quite normal.—Come right in, warm up a bit.—Oh, of course, yes, just a girl's whim; and what reason to fear murder now? That will amaze them, even Filippo.

Is that you, sallow face? *(The moon appears.)*

If the partisans of a republic were men, what a revolution there would be in the city tomorrow! But Piero is just ambitious; the Rucellai alone are worth something.—Oh, words, words, everlasting words! If there is someone up there, he must really be laughing at all of us. It really is very funny.—Oh, babbling mankind! Good for killing dead men! Good for battering down open doors! Helpless!

No, no, I won't take the lamp away!—I shall go straight for his heart. He shall see himself being killed... By Christ's blood, the people will be at their windows tomorrow.

I hope he has not contrived some new armor, some coat of mail. What a cursed invention! It is child's play to struggle with God and the devil; but to struggle with bits of metal hooked one around the other by the damned hand of an armorer! I shall come in after him; he will put his sword down here—or here—yes, on the sofa.—As for the matter of rolling the baldric around the hilt, that is easy. The easiest thing would if he should take it into his head to lie down; lie down, sit, or stand up? Sit, rather. I shall walk toward the door. Scoronconcolo is shut up in the closet. Then we come, we come; but I would not want him to have his back to us. I shall go straight up to him.—Come now, calm down! The hour will come.—I must go to a tavern; I did not notice that I am getting cold, I shall have a drink of something. No, I do not want to drink. Where the devil am I going, anyway? The taverns are closed.

Is she a good sort?—Oh, yes.—In her nightgown?—Oh, no, no, I do not think so.—Poor Caterina! It would be sad if my mother were to die from all this. But even if I had told her of my plan, what could I have done about it? Instead of comforting her that would have made her say, "Murder! murder!" until her final breath.

I do not know why I am pacing about, I am tired to death. *(He sits down.)*

Poor Filippo! The girl was radiantly beautiful. I sat down next to her once under a chestnut tree. How well she sewed with those little white hands! I have spent so many days sitting under the trees! Oh, what calm! The horizon at Cafaggiuolo![57] Giannetta, the housekeeper's little daughter, was so pretty drying her wash. She would chase away the goats that came and trod on her linen, spread out on the grass! The white goat would always come back with its long, slender legs. *(A clock strikes.)*

Oh, oh, I must go over there.—Good evening, darling; hah, clink your glass with Giomo.—Good wine! It would be amusing if he should happen to ask me if my room is secluded and whether the neighbors might hear anything. That would be amusing. Ha, it has been foreseen. Yes, it would be very funny if he happened to think of that.

I was mistaken about the time: it is only half past. What can that light be under the church portico? Someone is carving stones and moving them about. It seems these fellows are courageous when it comes to stone. See how they cut it and plunge their chisels in! They are making a crucifix; how bravely they are nailing it up! I would like to see their marble corpse suddenly grab them by the throat.

Well? Well? What now? I feel an incredible urge to dance. I think I would hop like a sparrow over all those great piles of rubble and girders if I let myself go. So, darling! Put on your brand new gloves, a finer outfit than that, tra, la, la! Put on your finery, the bride is beautiful. But let me whisper in your ear, watch out for her little knife. *(He runs out.)*

Scene 10.

The Duke's palace.

(The Duke, having supper; Giomo. Enter Cardinal Cibo.)

Cardinal Your Highness, beware of Lorenzo.

Duke So here you are, Cardinal! Sit down, have a glass of wine.

Cardinal Beware of Lorenzo, Duke. This evening he went and asked the Bishop of Marzi for permission to have post horses tonight.

Duke That is not possible.

Cardinal I heard it from the Bishop himself.

Duke Come, now! I tell you that I have good reason to know that it is not possible.

Cardinal It may be impossible to make you believe me. I have fulfilled my duty by warning you.

Duke Even if it should be true, what is so frightening about that? Perhaps he is going to Cafaggiuolo.

Cardinal What is frightening, my lord, is that as I crossed the square coming here I saw him with my own eyes, jumping up and down on beams and stones like a madman. I called him and I am obliged to admit that the look in his eyes horrified me. You may be sure that he is hatching some plan in his head for tonight.

Duke And why would such plans be dangerous to me?

Cardinal Must I say everything, even when speaking of your favorite? Let me tell you that he told two people I know, in public, on their terraces, that he would kill you tonight.

Duke Come on and have a glass of wine, Cardinal. Do you not know that Renzo is generally drunk by sunset? *(Enter Lord Maurizio.)*

Maurizio Your Highness, do not trust Lorenzo. He told three of my friends this evening that he wanted to kill you tonight.

Duke So, Lord Maurizio, you believe in fairy-tales, too? I thought you were more of a man than that.

Maurizio Your Highness knows that I am not one to be frightened without cause. I can prove what I say.

Duke Sit down, then, and have a drink with the Cardinal. I hope you won't mind if I go about my business. Well, darling, is it time already? *(Enter Lorenzo.)*

Lorenzo It is almost midnight.

Duke Have them give me my sable doublet.

Lorenzo Let's go quickly, your charmer may already be at the rendezvous.

Duke Which gloves should I wear? Those for war or those for love?

Lorenzo Those for love, your Highness.

Duke All right, I want to be a dashing suitor. *(Exeunt.)*

Maurizio What do you say to this, Cardinal?

Cardinal That God's will is done despite what men do. *(Exeunt.)*

Scene 11.

Lorenzo's bedroom.

(Enter the Duke and Lorenzo.)

Duke I am chilled to the bone—it really is cold out. *(He takes off his sword.)* Well, darling, what ever are you doing?

Lorenzo I am rolling your baldric around your sword and putting it under your pillow. It is always good to have a weapon ready at hand. *(He twists the baldric so as to prevent the sword from coming out of the scabbard.)*

Duke You know that I do not like talkative women, and I have heard that Caterina is a fine talker. To avoid conversation I am going to get into bed. By the way, why did you ask the Bishop of Marzi for post horses?

Lorenzo To go see my brother, who is quite ill according to what he writes me.

Duke Go and get your aunt, then.

Lorenzo Right away. *(Exit.)*

Duke *(alone)* It always has seemed quite senseless to me, and really worthy of a Frenchman, to court a woman who answers "yes" when you ask her "yes or no?" Today especially, after eating like three monks, I would be incapable of even saying, "My dear, my heart's desire" to the Infanta of Spain. I think I shall pretend to be asleep. That might perhaps be discourteous but it is convenient. *(He lies down.—Lorenzo comes back in, sword in hand.)*

Lorenzo Are you sleeping, my lord? *(He stabs him.)*

Duke Renzo, is that you?

Lorenzo Do not doubt it, my lord. *(He stabs him again. Enter Scoronconcolo.)*

Scoronc. Is it done?

Lorenzo Look, he bit my finger. I shall keep this bloody ring, this invaluable jewel, until I die.

Scoronc. Oh, my God, it is the Duke of Florence!

Lorenzo *(sitting on the window sill)* How beautiful the night is! The air is so pure! Breathe deeply, oh heart pierced by joy!

Scoronc. Come on, master, we have gone too far. We had better run away.

Lorenzo How sweetly scented the evening breeze is! The flowers in the meadows are opening. Oh, majestic nature! Oh, eternal rest!

Scoronc. The wind is going to chill the sweat that is streaming down your face. Come, my lord.

Lorenzo Oh, God of mercy! What a moment!

Scoronc. *(aside)* His heart is swelling strangely. As for me, I shall go first. *(He goes toward the door.)*

Lorenzo Wait, draw the curtains. Now give me the key to the room.

Scoronc. I hope the neighbors didn't hear anything!

Lorenzo Don't you remember? They are used to our noise. Come now, let's go. *(Exeunt.)*

ACT FIVE
Scene 1.

The Duke's palace.

(Enter Valori, Lord Maurizio and Guicciardini. A crowd of courtiers is milling about in the hall and surrounding area.)

Maurizio Giomo has not yet come back with his message. This is becoming more and more disturbing.

Guicciar. Here he is, coming into the hall. *(Enter Giomo.)*

Maurizio Well, what did you find out?

Giomo Nothing at all. *(Exit.)*

Guicciar. He won't answer; Cardinal Cibo is shut up in the Duke's study; he is the only one who gets any news. *(Enter another messenger.)* Well, have they found the Duke? Does anyone know where he is?

Messeng. I don't know. *(He goes into the study.)*

Valori What a terrible event this disappearance is, gentlemen! No news of the Duke. Didn't you say you saw him yesterday evening, Lord Maurizio? He didn't seem ill? *(Giomo comes back.)*

Giomo *(to Lord Maurizio)* I can tell you privately: the Duke has been murdered.

Maurizio Murdered! By whom? Where did you find him?

Giomo Where you had said: in Lorenzo's bedroom.

Maurizio Ha, by the devil! Does the Cardinal know?

Giomo Yes, your Excellency.

Maurizio What does he want to do? What can anyone do? The people are already gathering in a crowd in front of the palace. This whole dreadful affair has leaked out. We are dead men if it is confirmed. They will hack us to pieces. *(Servants bearing casks of wine and food go by the back of the stage.)*

Guicciar. What does that mean? Are they going to hand out food and drink to the people? *(A court nobleman enters.)*

Noble May the Duke be seen, my lords? This is a cousin of mine who has just arrived from Germany whom I wish to present to his Highness. Be so kind as to look favorably on him.

Guicciar. You answer him, Valori, I do not know what to tell him.

Valori The hall keeps filling up with these morning flatterers. They are waiting calmly to be admitted.

Maurizio *(to Giomo)* Has he been buried here?

Giomo Why, yes, in the sacristy. What do you expect? If the people learned of that death, they might cause a lot more. When it is time he will receive a public funeral. In the meanwhile, we took him away rolled up in a carpet.

Valori What is to become of us?

Several nobles *(coming up)* Shall we soon be allowed to pay our respects to his Highness? What do you think, gentlemen?

Cardinal *(entering)* Yes, gentlemen, you will be able to enter in an hour or two. The Duke spent the night at a masked ball and he is resting for the moment. *(Servants hang masquerade cloaks from the windows.)*

Courtiers Let us withdraw. The Duke is still in bed. He spent the night at the ball. *(The courtiers withdraw. Enter the Council of Eight.)*

Niccolini Well, Cardinal, what has been decided?

Cardinal *Primo avulso non deficit alter*
Aureus, et simili frondescit virga metallo.[58] *(Exit.)*

Niccolini That is quite marvelous. But what has been done? The Duke is dead. Another one must be elected and as quickly as possible. If we don't have a Duke this evening or tomorrow, we are done for. The people are like water about to boil at this very moment.

Vettori I propose Ottaviano de' Medici.

Capponi Why? He is not the first in line by blood.

Acciaiuoli What about taking the Cardinal?

Maurizio Are you joking?

Ruccellai Why indeed shouldn't you take the Cardinal? You are allowing him to act as the sole judge in this matter in disregard of all the laws.

Vettori He is a man who is capable of managing the matter quite well.

Ruccellai Then he should have the Pope give him the order.

Vettori That is what he has done. The Pope sent his authorization by a courier that the Cardinal dispatched during the night.

Ruccellai You mean by a bird, I suppose. A courier has to take enough time to go in the first place before he takes enough time to come back. Are we being treated like children?

Canigiani *(coming up)* Gentlemen, if you will listen to me, here is what we shall do: we'll elect his[59] illegitimate son, Giuliano, as Duke of Florence.

Ruccellai Bravo! A five-year-old child! He is five, isn't he, Canigiani?

Guicciar. *(softly)* Can't you see what he is doing? It is the Cardinal who put that foolish proposition into his head. Cibo would be regent and the child would eat cookies.

Ruccellai This is shameful. I shall leave the room if there is any more such talk.

Corsi *(entering)* Gentlemen, the Cardinal has just written to Cosimo de' Medici.

Eight Without consulting us?

Corsi The Cardinal has also written to the military commanders in Pisa, Arezzo, and Pistoia. Giacomo de' Medici will be here tomorrow with as many men as possible. Alessandro Vitelli[60] is already in the fortress with the entire garrison. As for Lorenzo, three couriers have been sent out to reach him.

Ruccellai Your Cardinal should name himself Duke right off; it would be quicker that way.

Corsi I have been ordered to request you to vote on Cosimo de' Medici's election with the interim title of Governor of the Florentine Republic.

Giomo *(to servants crossing the room)* Spread sand around the door and don't spare the wine or anything else.

Ruccellai The poor people! What a bunch of onlookers you are being made into!

Maurizio Come now, gentlemen, let us vote. Here are your ballots.

Vettori Cosimo is the first in line after Alessandro in point of fact. He is his closest relation.

Acciaiuoli What kind of man is he? I hardly know him.

Corsi He is the finest prince one could find.

Guicciar. Ha, ha, not quite. It would be truer if you said the vaguest and the most ceremonious of princes.

Maurizio Your ballots, gentlemen.

Ruccellai I am opposed to this vote, positively and in the name of all the citizens.

Vettori Why?

Ruccellai The Republic has no more need for princes, dukes, or lords. Here is my ballot. *(He holds up his blank ballot.)*

Vettori Yours is only one vote. We shall manage without you.

Ruccellai Farewell, then. I wash my hands of it.

Guicciar. *(running after him)* Oh, my God, Palla, don't be so impetuous!

Ruccellai Leave me alone. I am over sixty-two years old, so you cannot do me great harm now. *(Exit.)*

Niccolini Your ballots, gentlemen. *(He unfolds the ballots that have been thrown into a hat.)* It is unanimous. Has the courier left for Trebbio?

Corsi Yes, your Excellency. Cosimo will be here tomorrow before noon unless he refuses.

Vettori Why should he refuse?

Niccolini Oh, my God, if he should refuse what would become of us? It is fifteen leagues from here to Trebbio to find Cosimo and as many back; that would be a whole day wasted. We ought to have chosen someone closer by.

Vettori What do you want? Our vote has been cast and it is likely he will accept. All this is most bewildering. *(Exeunt.)*

Scene 2.

In Venice.

(Filippo Strozzi, in his study.)

Filippo I was certain of it.—Piero has been in contact with the King of France. Now he has been set at the head of some sort of army, and he is ready to put the town to the torch and the sword. And that is all that the poor name of Strozzi, which was respected for so long, has accomplished! It will have produced one rebel and two or three massacres. Oh, my Luisa! You are sleeping in peace beneath the earth; oblivion is all around you as it is within you, down in the sad valley where I left you. *(There is a knock at the door.)* Come in. *(Enter Lorenzo.)*

Lorenzo Filippo, I have brought you the most beautiful jewel in your crown.

Filippo What is that you have thrown down there? A key?

Lorenzo This is the key to my bedroom and in my bedroom is Alessandro de' Medici, who died by this hand.

Filippo Is that really true? It is incredible.

Lorenzo You can believe it if you want to. You will hear about it from others than me.

Filippo *(taking the key)* Alessandro is dead! Is that possible?

Lorenzo What would you say if the republicans offered to make you Duke in his place?

Filippo I would refuse, my friend.

Lorenzo Is that really true? It is incredible.

Filippo Why? It is quite simple for me.

Lorenzo As it is for me to kill Alessandro. Why won't you believe me?

Filippo Oh, you are our new Brutus! I believe you and I embrace you. So liberty has been saved! Yes, I believe you, you are what you told me you were. Give me your hand. The Duke is dead! Oh, there is no hatred in my joy; there is only the purest, the most holy love for my country. I take God as my witness.

Lorenzo Come now, calm down. Nothing has been saved except my skin, and the Bishop of Marzi's horses have broken my back.

Filippo Haven't you informed our friends? Haven't they taken up their swords by this time?

Lorenzo I did inform them. I knocked on all the republican doors with the persistence of a mendicant friar. I told them to shine up their swords, and that Alessandro would be dead by the time they awoke. I think that, by this time, they have reawakened several times and gone back to sleep each time. But to tell the truth, that is all I think.

Filippo Did you inform the Pazzi? Did you tell Corsini?

Lorenzo Everyone. I think I might have said it to the moon, I was so sure no one would listen.

Filippo What do you mean?

Lorenzo I mean that they shrugged their shoulders and went back to their dinners, their dice cups and their wives.

Filippo But didn't you explain the matter to them?

Lorenzo What the deuce did you want me to explain? Do you think I had an hour to waste with each of them? I told them: Be prepared, and then I struck my blow.

Filippo So you think the Pazzi are doing nothing? How do you know? You have had no news since you left, and you have been on the road for several days.

Lorenzo I think the Pazzi are doing something; I think they are practicing dueling in their antechamber and taking a drink of wine from time to time when their throats get dry.

Filippo You are sticking to your wager. Didn't you want to bet me what you have just said? Don't worry, I have hopes of better.

Lorenzo I am not worried; I am calmer than I can say.

Filippo Why didn't you go out holding the Duke's head in your hand? The people would have followed you as their savior and chief.

Lorenzo I left the stag to the hounds; they can do as they want with the spoils.

Filippo You would have worshipped mankind if you didn't have such scorn for it.

Lorenzo I don't have scorn for men; I just know them. I am quite convinced that there are a very few truly wicked ones, many cowardly ones and a great number of indifferent ones. There are also some savage ones, like the inhabitants of Pistoia, who took advantage of this business to slit all their chancellors' throats in the streets in broad daylight. I learned of that less than an hour ago.

Filippo I am filled with joy and hope. My heart is throbbing in spite of myself.

Lorenzo I am happy for you.

Filippo Since you have not heard anything, why do you speak that way? Certainly, all men are not capable of great deeds, but they are all impressed by great deeds. Would you deny the history of the entire world? Of course, it takes a spark to set a forest on fire; but the spark may come from a rock and the forest catches fire. In the same way, the flash of a single sword can light up an entire century.

Lorenzo I don't deny history. I just wasn't there.

Filippo Let me call you Brutus. If I am a dreamer, let me have that dream. Oh, my friends, my compatriots, you can make a fine death-bed for old Strozzi if you only wish!

Lorenzo Why are you opening the window?

Filippo Don't you see the courier galloping down that road toward us? My Brutus, my great Lorenzo, freedom is in the air! I feel it, I can breathe it.

Lorenzo Filippo! Filippo! None of that. Shut your window, all these words hurt me.

Filippo I think there is a crowd gathering down in the street. A town crier is reading a proclamation. Ho, Giovanni! Go buy that crier's paper.

Lorenzo Oh, God! Oh, God!

Filippo You have grown as pale as death. What is the matter with you?

Lorenzo Didn't you hear? *(A servant enters, bringing the proclamation.)*

Filippo No. Come read the proclamation that was being announced in the street.

Lorenzo "The Council of Eight of Florence promises any man, noble or commoner, who kills Lorenzo de' Medici, a traitor to his country and the assassin of his master, wherever it may be and however it may be done, within the borders of all Italy, the following: 1° four thousand gold florins with none withheld; 2° an income of one hundred gold florins per year for the remainder of his life and to his direct heirs after his death; 3° permission to exercise any office, to possess any living or privilege of the state despite his birth if he is a commoner; 4° perpetual pardon for all his transgressions, past and future, ordinary and extraordinary.

Signed by the hand of the
Eight."

Well, Filippo, a little while ago you wouldn't believe that I killed Alessandro? Now you see that I did.

Filippo Be still! Someone is coming up the stairs. Hide in this room. *(Exeunt.)*

Scene 3.

Florence.—A street.

(Enter two noblemen.)

First nob. Isn't that Marquis Cibo going by? I believe he is walking arm in arm with his wife. *(The Marquis and the Marquise go by.)*

Second nob. It would seem that the good Marquis doesn't have a vindictive nature. Everyone in Florence knows that his wife was the late Duke's mistress.

First nob. They seem to have made up. I thought I saw them holding hands.

Second nob. Truly a jewel among husbands! You have to have a strong stomach to swallow an outrage as great as that.

First nob. I know people are talking,— but I don't advise you to go and mention it to the Marquis himself. He is quite skilled in all weapons, and people who make jokes may end up six feet under in his garden.

Second nob. Oh, if he is an eccentric, that is his business. *(Exeunt.)*

Scene 4.

An inn.

(Enter Piero Strozzi and a messenger.)

Piero Are those his own words?

Messenger Yes, your Excellency. Those are the very words the king spoke.

Piero You may go. *(Exit the messenger.)* The King of France protecting freedom in Italy is just like a highway robber protecting a pretty traveling lady from another robber. He defends her, and then he rapes her. Well, whatever may be, a way is opening up before me on which there are more good seeds than soil. A curse on Lorenzaccio for getting the idea to make a name for himself! My revenge has slipped from my fingers like a skittish bird. I cannot think up anything here that is worthy of me. Let us go storm the town, and then let us forget about these weaklings, who think of nothing but my father's name and stare at me all day long to find out how I resemble him. I was born for better things than to become a bandit chief. *(Exit.)*

Scene 5.

A square—Florence.

(The goldsmith and the silk merchant, seated.)

Merchant Now pay attention to what I am saying. Mark my words. The late Duke Alessandro was killed in the year 1536, which is the very year in which we are now living. So follow me carefully. Now he was killed in the year 1536; that much has been done. He was twenty-six years old; you see what I mean? But that is nothing yet. Now, he was twenty-six, right? He died on the 6th of the month. Ha! ha! Did you realize that: was it not precisely on the 6th that he died? Now, listen. He died at midnight, the sixth hour of the night. What do you think of that, Mondella, old friend? If that isn't extraordinary, I don't know what is. So, he died at the sixth hour of the night. Hush! Do not say a thing yet. He had six wounds. Well, does that strike you now? He had six wounds, in the sixth hour of the night, on the sixth of the month, at the age of twenty-six, in the year 1536. Now, just one word more: He had reigned for six years.[61]

Goldsmith What kind of balderdash are you feeding me, neighbor?

Merchant What! So, are you totally incapable of figuring it out? Don't you see what comes of the supernatural combinations I have the honor to explain to you?

Goldsmith No, to tell the truth. I do not see what comes of it.

Merchant You don't see? Is it really possible for you not to see, neighbor?

Goldsmith I do not see in the least what comes of all that. What good can it possibly do us?

Merchant What comes of it is that six Sixes came together in Alessandro's death. Shh! Do not tell anyone that you heard this from me. You know that I am considered a wise and prudent man; in the name of all the saints, you must not wrong me! The matter is far graver than people think. I am telling you this as a friend.

Goldsmith Go jump in the lake. I may be an old man, but I am not yet an old woman. Cosimo arrives today, that is the clearest thing that comes out of this business. During your night of the six Sixes, a fine spinner of empty words has suddenly sprouted up among us. Oh, isn't that shameful, by heaven! My workers, right down to the least ones, rapped their tools on their tables when they saw the Eight ride by, neighbor, and they shouted out to them: "If you will not or cannot do anything, call on us and we will."

Merchant Yours aren't the only ones who shouted. There is a clamor in the city such as I have never before heard or even heard about.

Goldsmith People are calling for a vote.[62] Some of them are running after the soldiers, others after the wine that is being distributed and they are filling their mouths and brains with it so as to lose what little common sense and decent speech might be left in them.

Merchant Some of them wanted to resurrect the Council and freely elect a Gonfalonier as they used to.

Goldsmith As you say, some of them wanted to. But none of them did anything. In spite of my years, I went to the New Market and got a pike thrust into my leg because I was calling for a vote. Not a soul came to my aid. Only the students stuck their noses out.

Merchant I believe you. Do you know what they are saying, neighbor? They are saying that the governor of the Fortress, Roberto Corsini, went yesterday to the meeting of the republicans at the Salviati palace.

Goldsmith That is absolutely true. He offered to hand the fortress over to the friends of liberty along with the supplies, the keys and all the rest.

Merchant And did he do that, neighbor? Did he? It is high treason.

Goldsmith Oh, well, yes, they made a lot of noise, drank mulled wine and broke some windows. But the good man's proposal was not even listened to. Since they did not dare do what he wanted, they said they were suspicious of him and did not trust in the genuineness of his offers. God damn it to hell! It makes me so angry! Look, here come some couriers from Trebbio; Cosimo is not far off. Good night, neighbor, I am getting itchy, I have to go to the palace. *(Exit.)*

Merchant Wait a minute, neighbor; I'll go with you. *(Exit. Enter a tutor with a Salviati child and another with a Strozzi child.)*

First tutor *Sapientissime doctor*, how is your lordship feeling? Is the treasure of your precious health in its right state, and is your equilibrium remaining correct during the tempests we are now experiencing?

Second tutor My learned Doctor, so erudite and fruitful an encounter as ours is a momentous thing on this, our cracked and careworn soil. Suffer me to press that mighty hand from which so many of our language's masterpieces have issued forth. Admit it, you have just recently written a sonnet.

Salviati child You good-for-nothing Strozzi!

Strozzi child Your father got beaten up, Salviati!

First tutor Can that poor frolic of our muse have risen even up to you, a man of such broad, austere and meticulous art? Can eyes such as yours, which stir such filigreed, phosphorescent horizons, have deigned to note the perhaps bizarre and audacious fumes of a refulgent imagination?

Second tutor Oh, if you love art and ourselves, please deign to recite your sonnet for us. The entire city has nothing but your sonnet on its mind.

First tutor You may perhaps be surprised that I, who started out singing of the monarchy to a certain extent, now appear to be singing of the republic.

Salviati child Stop kicking me, Strozzi.

Strozzi child Take this, you Salviati bastard, here are a couple more.

First tutor Here is the poem:

We sing of freedom, with its bitter blooms...

Salviati child Make that little guttersnipe stop it, sir. He is a cutthroat. All the Strozzi are cutthroats.

Second tutor Come, come, little boy, behave yourself.

Strozzi child You sneak! Take this, you wretch, you can bring it to your father and tell him to put it with the whipping he got from Piero

Strozzi, you poisonous pain in the neck! You are all a bunch of poisoners.

First tutor Will you be still, you little rascal! *(He strikes him.)*

Strozzi child Ouch! He hit me.

First tutor We sing of freedom, with its bitter blooms,
Which flow'r anew 'neath newly azure heav'ns.

Strozzi child Ouch! He skinned my ear.

Second tutor You struck him too hard, my friend. *(The Strozzi child thrashes the Salviati child.)*

First tutor Well, what does this mean?

Second tutor I pray you, please continue.

First tutor With pleasure, but these children keep on fighting. *(The children go out fighting. The tutors follow them.)*

Scene 6.[63]

Florence. A street.

(Enter students and soldiers.)

A student Since the nobles can do nothing but talk, it is up to us to act. Hey, we want to vote![64] Citizens of Florence, we mustn't let them choose a Duke without us voting.

A soldier You won't get to vote. Back away.

Student Citizens, come over here. Your rights are not being recognized, the people are being insulted. *(A great tumult.)*

Soldiers Watch out! Back off.

Other student We are willing to die for our rights.

Soldier Die, then. *(He strikes him.)*

Student Avenge me, Roberto, and look after my mother. *(He dies.— The students attack the soldiers; they go off fighting.)*

Scene 7.

Venice. Strozzi's study.

(Enter Filippo and Lorenzo, who is holding a letter.)

Lorenzo This letter here says my mother has died. Come and take a walk with me, Filippo.

Filippo I beg you, my friend, do not tempt fate. You come in and out all the time as if that death proclamation did not exist.

Lorenzo At the time when I was going to kill Clement VII, a price was put on my head in Rome. It is natural for that to be so in all of Italy now that I have killed Alessandro. If I left Italy, I would soon be heralded by trumpets through all of Europe; and on my death the Lord in heaven will not fail to post my eternal damnation on all the street corners of eternity.

Filippo Your humor is as melancholy as the night. You have not changed, Lorenzo.

Lorenzo No, that is true. I am wearing the same clothes, I still walk on my legs and I yawn with my mouth. Only a trifle has changed in me: I am hollower and emptier than a tin statue.

Filippo Let us leave together. Become a man again. You have done a great deal but you are still young.

Lorenzo I am older than Saturn's great-grandfather. Please, come and take a walk with me.

Filippo Your mind tortures itself through inactivity. That is your trouble. You have your flaws, my friend.

Lorenzo I agree. It is a great flaw on my part that the republicans did nothing in Florence, that a hundred or so young brave, determined students got massacred in vain, that Cosimo, a milksop, has been unanimously elected. Oh, I admit it, these are unforgiveable flaws; they make me look very bad indeed.

Filippo Let us not argue over an event that has not yet run its course. The important thing is to leave Italy. Your time on earth is not yet over.

Lorenzo I was a killing-machine, but for one killing only.

Filippo Have you known happiness from nothing but that murder? Even if you were henceforth to become just an honest man or an artist, why should you want to die?

Lorenzo I can only repeat my own words: Filippo, I was honest. Perhaps I might go back to that if it weren't for the boredom that consumes me. I still like wine and women: that is enough, indeed, to make me into a wastrel, but it is not enough to make me feel like being one. Let us go out, I beg you.

Filippo You are going to get yourself killed with all these walks.

Lorenzo It amuses me to see them. The reward is so great that it almost makes them brave. Yesterday a big, strapping fellow with bare legs followed me for a whole quarter of an hour on the waterfront, but he couldn't make up his mind to kill me. The poor man was carrying some kind of knife as long as a roasting-spit. He kept looking at it so glumly, I could not help pitying him. Perhaps he was a family man, starving.

Filippo Oh, Lorenzo, Lorenzo! Your heart is very sick. He was probably an honest man. Why should you impute respect for the unfortunate to people's cowardice?

Lorenzo Impute it to whatever you want. I am going for a walk on the Rialto. *(Exit.)*

Filippo *(alone)* I must have one of my men follow him. Ho, there, Giovanni! Pippo! Hey! *(enter a servant)* Take a sword and go with one of your comrades. Follow Messire Lorenzo at a suitable distance so you can help him out in case he is attacked.

Giovanni Yes, my lord. *(Enter Pippo.)*

Pippo My lord, Lorenzo is dead. A man was hiding behind the door and he struck him from behind as he went out.

Filippo Let us run quickly, perhaps he is only wounded.

Pippo Don't you see that crowd? The people ran up and grabbed him. God of mercy, they are throwing him into the lagoon!

Filippo Oh, how horrible! What, not even a grave? *(Exit.)*

Scene 8.

Florence.—The main square. Grandstands are filled with people. (The populace is running in all directions.)

People It's a vote! It's a vote![65] He is Duke! It's a vote! He is Duke!

Soldiers Make way, rabble!

Cardinal *(on a dais, to Cosimo de' Medici)* My lord, you are Duke of Florence. Before receiving from my hands the crown that the Pope and the Emperor have entrusted me with granting you, I have been commanded to make you swear to do four things.

Cosimo What are they, Cardinal?

Cardinal To carry out justice without restriction; never to attempt anything against Charles the Fifth's authority; to avenge the death of Alessandro; and to protect his illegitimate children, signor Giulio and signora Giulia.

Cosimo How should I pronounce this oath?

Cardinal On the Gospel.

Cosimo I swear it to God and to you, Cardinal. Now give me your hand. *(They walk toward the populace. Cosimo is heard speaking in the distance.)*

"Most noble and mighty lords. The thanks that I wish to offer to your most illustrious and gracious lordships for the very high privilege that I owe you are nothing else than my commitment that, young as I am, I find a sweet burden, to keep forever in mind, along with the fear of God, decency and justice and the goal of offending no man either in his property or in his honor; and in my governing of state affairs never to swerve from the counsel and judgment of your most wise and judicious lordships, to whom I offer myself completely and pay my most devout respects."[66]

The End

Notes

1 As for *Andrea del Sarto*, it has been set to music by the composer Daniel-Lesur, first (in 1947) as incidental music, then as a symphonic poem and finally as a lyric drama, premiered by the Marseilles Opera in 1969.

2 Paul Dimoff analyzed *Lorenzaccio*'s debt to the unfinished *scène historique* of Musset's lover, George Sand, "Une Conspiration en 1537," in *La Genèse de Lorenzaccio*, Paris, 1964.

3 See Paul de Musset, *Biographie d'Alfred de Musset*, in Musset, *Œuvres complètes*, Paris, 1963, p. 28.

4 First published in *Revue des deux mondes*, 15 May 1838, then collected in Musset's *Nouvelles* in 1848.

5 Since Andrea's dates are 1486-1530, Michelangelo, who died in 1564, was still alive at the time of Musset's protagonist's death.

6 Not in 1537, as in George Sand's title for her *scène historique*.

7 See my *Theater of Solitude. The Drama of Alfred de Musset*, chapter 6, for a more complete analysis of the play's action.

8 The Italian suffix *-accio* traditionally applied to Lorenzo is pejorative. Curiously, Alexandre Dumas *père* entitled his play on the same subject *Lorenzino*, emphasizing, as does Musset, Lorenzo's small stature, which—along with Lorenzo's apparent sexual ambivalence and his lack of "masculine" courage—may explain why the role was played by female actors, starting with Sarah Bernhardt, for over half a century.

9 I do not share the view expressed in Bernard Masson's otherwise exemplary study, *Musset et le théâtre intérieur* (see in particular p. 394), that the painter, Tebaldeo, as well as other young figures is in some way spared from the general cynicism of the play and represents a triumph of art over crass political realism.

10 See "Un souper chez Rachel," Musset's humorous account of his first visit to Rachel's house in 1838, written as a letter to his friend and former mistress, Mme Jaubert, and published posthumously in *Œuvres complètes* (1963), p. 910.

Notes to *Andrea del Sarto*

1 Cf. Alfred de Musset, *Théâtre complet*, Paris, 1958, p. 1186.

2 See "Selected Bibliography." Musset's later interest in seeing the play performed on the stage is suggested, however, by his placing it among the "Comédies et Proverbes" already at the time of the 1840 Charpentier edition of his "complete" works and his dropping of the title *Théâtre dans un fauteuil* (see Gastinel, *Les Deux "André del Sarto"*, pp. 43-44).

3 Cf. "Selected Bibliography."

4 Paul de Musset, *Biographie d'Alfred de Musset*, in Alfred de Musset, *Œuvres complètes*, Paris, 1963, p. 28..

5 In *Lorenzaccio* Musset also telescopes the last days of his hero, Lorenzo de' Medici, making him die shortly after his assassination of Duke Alessandro, rather than several years later as in historical reality.

6 For this "regularized" version of the play, performed at the Odéon, see the edition referred to in note 1 above, pp. 20-48, as well as Pierre Gastinel's *"thèse complémentaire," Les Deux "André del Sarto" d'Alfred de Musset.* In any case, Musset's original text already telescoped the action of the drama into a brief period of time, following French neo-classical tradition.

7 This is the text printed in *Œuvres complètes de A. de Musset. Comédies et Proverbes, texte établi et présenté par Pierre Gastinel*, v. 1, Paris: Société les Belles Lettres, 1952.

8 Gremio refers to her in French as "Madame Lucrèce"; his tone throughout the play, however, appears to me too "popular" to use that title in English.

9 Although "like" is grammatically incorrect here, it seems to me more suitable to Gremio's diction than "as."

10 Michelangelo was actually very much alive then and died only in 1564, more than thirty years after Andrea del Sarto: this is one of Musset's alterations of historical truth in the service of his dramatic vision. When he revised the play for production in 1848, he substituted throughout the name of Raphael, who died in 1520, for that of Michelangelo.

11 Iacopo Carucci, usually called *Il Pontormo* (1494-1556), a disciple of Michelangelo, was in fact a pupil and assistant of Andrea del Sarto until 1518; his teacher is said to have treated him harshly, out of jealousy, when he reached independence. In his maturity Pontormo was one of the dominant figures of the mannerist school. Filhol speaks disapprovingly of "son caractère bisarre [*sic*] et indécis."

12 The great German painter (1471-1538) was another of Pontormo's inspirations.

13 See above, note 10.

14 Andrea had been entrusted by Francis the First with a large sum of money on his return from France to Florence to acquire art works for the king. He squandered it for the sake of his wife, Lucrezia del Fede.

15 This praise of Francis the First and the French renaissance gives retrospective evidence of the play's national origins. Such sentiments were expressed more openly still in Filhol's account, which refers to renaissance France as "une nation généreuse, dont le noble désintéressement l'avait [i.e., Andrea del Sarto] si bien accueilli."

16 Musset here follows the authors of the *Dictionnaire des Arts*, as cited by Filhol: Andrea del Sarto is said to have received payment in grain for a painting of the Holy Family, part of his fresco decorations for the porch of the Annunciation church.

17 Cf. note 10.

18 Cf. note 14.

19 Andrea del Sarto had been treated with great honor by King Francis and his court in 1518.

20 "Charity" is one of three Andrea del Sarto paintings among the engravings in Filhol's *Musée* (vol. 8, 85th "*livraison*," plate 1), although it is not exactly as described here. Filhol says of it "This picture is one of the most beautiful works from the brush of this painter, who was as famous as he was ill-fated." Filhol points out that it was painted shortly before Andrea's death and several years after the time of his abuse of the French king's funds, one of two commissions from Giovan Battista della Palla, who was acting on behalf of King Francis, the painting's eventual owner.

21 This is a quality that both Vasari and Filhol ascribe to Andrea del Sarto.

22 Andrea's name ("del Sarto") reflects the fact that his father was a tailor. In his notices on the painter, Filhol gives his name as Andrea Vannuchi, "called Del Sarto." Elsewhere (see, for example, Musset, *Théâtre complet*, Paris, 1958, p. 1187) he is identified as Andrea d'Agnolo di Francesco del Luca, "called Andrea del Sarto."

Notes to *Lorenzaccio*

1 Sandeau later gave his copy of it to another of his mistresses, the celebrated actress Marie Dorval…

2 Although George Sand referred to him in her *scène historique* as "Grand Duke," a title only later accorded to the Duke of Florence, Musset restored him to his proper rank

3 Lorenzo, who also had a claim to the throne of Florence, was alternately referred to as "Lorenzino" (as in Dumas's play; the diminutive suffix "-ino" refers to his stature) and "Lorenzaccio," the pejorative suffix seeming to refer here both to his lifestyle and to his regicide.

4 This historical character, who plays such a significant role in Musset's drama, is not to be found in Sand, although Varchi mentions him; neither is his equally important sister-in-law, the Marquise Ricciarda Cibo.

5 Instead of "Marquess" and "Marchioness," the British equivalents of this character's and his wife's titles, I prefer "Marquis" and "Marquise," which are more familiar in America.

6 A common shortening of the name Bartolomeo in renaissance Italy.

7 Like the Cibos, this all-important character and his family do not figure in George Sand's *scène historique*, which concentrates solely on the central plot, Lorenzo's assassination of Alessandro.

8 The Ruccellai, like the Salviati and the Pazzi families, (as well as the Strozzi family mentioned above) were among the most powerful and influential in Florence.

9 This character was invented by Musset to represent the artists of Lorenzo's time in Florence. Cf. the almost contemporaneous events and comments in *Andrea del Sarto*.

10 George Sand gives his true name ("Scoronconcolo" being a nickname) as "Michel del Favolaccino," following a typographical error in her edition of Varchi; other editions refer to him as "Michele del Tovalaccino."

11 George Sand's misreading of Varchi's text was continued by Musset, who here has conflated two of Alexander's henchmen: Giomo and "the Hungarian." On this model Sand also created another squire for Alessandro, "Fernando the Andalusian."

12 The Soderini were one of the city's most powerful families. In recent years Piero Soderini had served a lengthy term as Gonfalonier of the Florentine Republic, until the restoration of the Medici to power; his brother, Francesco, was Archbishop of Volterra.

13 Sand calls her "Madonna Catterina, Lorenzo's sister." In fact, she was said by Varchi to be Lorenzo's "maternal aunt"; but other sources refer to her as his sister, and she calls Maria Soderini "mother" in I, vi, and II, iv, although Maria says that Lorenzo is Caterina's nephew.

14 Although George Sand's *scène historique* was entitled *Une Conspiration en 1537*, the date of the action was actually 1536. Like Musset's silk merchant in Act V, Scene V, Varchi makes much of the fact that Alessandro was murdered in his 26th year, in 1536, on the 6th of the month, at the 6th hour of the night, with 6 wounds, in the 6th year of his reign, the "six sixes" thus conspiring in his death.

15 These and other bourgeois characters, who act as a kind of chorus, were invented by Musset.

16 Charles V, Holy Roman Emperor from 1519 to 1556. He abdicated the throne two years before his death.

17 Alessandro was suspected of being responsible for the death by poisoning of his cousin and former rival for the throne of Florence, Ippolito de' Medici.

18 Musset corrects Sand's erroneous reference to this Pope as Clement VII, who had died in 1534 and been succeeded by Paul III.

19 Alessandro's interest in horses is as strong as his pursuit of women and his vocabulary often seems interchangeable for the two subjects.

20 Duke, in fact; but his power over Florence is absolute.

21 I.e., Lorenzaccio.

22 Varchi mentions this event (Book XV, vol. V). It actually took place several years earlier.

23 I.e., Pope Paul III.

24 According to Dimoff (*Genèse*, p. 223), Pietro Farnese's ill-treatment of Cosimo Gheri da Pistoia, the Bishop of Fano, actually occurred in 1538, after Alessandro's death.

25 It is interesting to note that Musset, who was himself a dandy, often employed the image of clothing to denote vanity, superficiality, and emptiness: cf. II, iv, along with *Fantasio*, I, ii.

26 Since Alessandro was the illegitimate son of Lorenzo de' Medici and a woman considered a harlot, Musset portrays him as particularly sensitive to this insult.

27 This would seem to be the one near Florence on the left bank of the Arno, and not the famous Benedictine monastery, Monteoliveto Maggiore, near Buonconvento, south of Siena.

28 Benvenuto Cellini, the renaissance sculptor (1500-1571), figured as a character in the plans for *Lorenzaccio* as well as in a written-out scene that Musset discarded: the artist enters Alessandro's room to give him a medallion that he has executed and finds him and Lorenzo asleep together (see Dimoff, pp. 169-175).

29 This reference to student insurrections is one link between *Lorenzaccio* and the political events surrounding the establishment of the "July Monarchy" in France in 1830.

30 Emperor Charles V and Pope Clement VII's meeting in Bologna actually took place in 1532, well after Alessandro's installation as Duke.

31 The Prior of Capua, a priest, is Leone Strozzi, Filippo's son and Luisa's brother.

32 A parody of these sentiments voiced by the Prince of Mantua in *Fantasio* (II, ii) reinforces the translator's feeling that Freccia is not

intended as an antidote through art to the prevailing pessimism of Musset's drama.

33 Musset's very real veneration of Raphael and Michelangelo permeates *Andrea del Sarto*. But Freccia's pietism is not treated kindly in any of the author's youthful works.

34 In Musset's, as in the minds of other educated Frenchmen, this statement would probably recall a celebrated beating that Voltaire received at the hands of a nobleman's lackeys.

35 Cibo's interest, not aroused by Ricciarda's words of political and religious rebelliousness, is suddenly piqued by mention of the Duke's amorous attentions, although she pretends not to notice.

36 The story of Lucius Junius Brutus's overthrow of the Roman monarchy after the rape of Lucretia, the wife of Collatinus, by Sextus Tarquin, is told by Livy in book I, chaps. 58-60, of his *History of Rome*. Its relevance to the story of Lorenzaccio is enhanced by the fact that Brutus feigned idiocy in order to accomplish his act.

37 For Lorenzo to name Tarquin a "Duke" here suggests the parallel the author sees between his contemplated act and Roman history.

38 Maria, who has been addressing Lorenzo as "vous" earlier in this scene, begins to address him with the intimate "tu" here, no doubt in consequence of her evocation of Lorenzo's childhood; she has used the "tu" form in all her scenes with Caterina, who uses the more formal and respectful "vous" with her. These variations, typical and significant in most languages, cannot be rendered directly in modern English, which has only a single second person pronoun and verb form.

39 Caterina is Lorenzo's aunt (although she refers to Maria as "mother"), yet he uses the "tu" form with her, while she addresses him more formally as "vous."

40 Bindo, who (as Lorenzo's uncle) has begun the scene addressing Lorenzo with the familiar "tu," uses the more formal "vous" in this speech, returning to the "tu" after Lorenzo's "insolence."

41 Cf. note 25.

42 Lorenzo's change of the subject at this point to distract the Duke from his aunt is illustrative of the process by which his original idealistic intentions have been modified by reality. His later characterization of

Strozzi as a "boor," which can be understood as applying to the Duke himself, further illustrates the tight-rope on which he finds himself.

43 According to Varchi, Luisa was already married to a Capponi and Caterina, Lorenzo's aunt, was married to a Ginori; but Musset's Romantic psychology required that they be virginal figures of feminine purity. Filippo reveals both ivory-tower aloofness and aristocratic pride in this speech.

44 Cf. note 42.

45 Count Ugolino, evoked in his delirium by Lorenzo, is portrayed in Dante's *Inferno* (Canto 33) among the traitors trapped in ice, eternally devouring the skull of his arch-enemy, Ruggiero Ubaldini, archbishop of Pisa, who had locked him up with his sons and grandsons in a tower, where Ugolino had been reduced by hunger to cannibalism.

46 Evidently the aim of the entire excercise.

47 As in the case of Gremio in *Andrea del Sarto*, the verbal style of the character suggests this ungrammatical usage.

48 The Pazzi family was one of Florence's oldest and most influential. In 1478 it had been involved in an ill-fated conspiracy against the Medici; this inspired Vittorio Alfieri's verse tragedy, *La Congiura dei Pazzi*, which Musset is thought to have read.

49 The Council of Eight (*Otto di Guardia*) exercised judicial authority in Florence.

50 This reference to "patriotic banquets" sounds more like Musset's Paris (cf. also Flaubert's novel, *L'Education sentimentale*) than renaissance Florence; it is one of several passages that link his play with contemporary French history.

51 Harmodius and Aristogiton were Athenian youths who assassinated the tyrant Hipparchus. They were later venerated by Athenians as martyrs to freedom.

52 Musset is referring here to the earlier Lucius Junius Brutus and not to Julius Cæsar's assassin, Marcus Junius Brutus.

53 Herostratus set fire to the Temple of Diana in Ephesus in order to achieve personal renown.

54 The French recalls the expression "La belle jambe [que cela me fait]!," widely used to signify "I couldn't care less" or "What difference does that make [to me]?" In any case, a reference to a woman's—as opposed to a man's—leg would certainly seem shocking to the public of Musset's time.

55 Cf. note 36.

56 Deianira offered a poisoned robe given her by the dying centaur Nessus to her husband, Hercules, who died in agony while wearing it.

57 Benedetto Varchi mentions in *Storia Fiorentina* Lorenzo's villa at Cafaggiuolo, as well as his requesting post horses of the Bishop of Marzi to go see his brother there (*Lorenzaccio*, IV, x).

58 The Cardinal is citing a verse from Virgil's *Æneid*, VI, 143-144: "When the first [branch] is torn off, another golden one is not lacking, and the twig grows leaves of a similar metal."

59 Most editions of the play have the first-person possessive adjective *mon* ("my") here; historical texts make it clear that this is a misreading.

60 Alessandro Vitelli was a well-known condottiere.

61 These numerical coincidences are cited in Varchi's chronicle (cf. note 14).

62 In the text, "balls" (see also below). Musset evidently misunderstood Varchi's text, which referred to the Medici's heraldic shield (it contained six balls: *tourteaux* in French; not, as in Musset's text, *boules*); this was not a reference to a method of voting (cf. the English expression, "to blackball").

63 This scene, omitted from the 1853 and 1856 editions, is not contained in all modern texts of the play.

64 See note 62.

65 See note 62.

66 Musset translated this speech of Cosimo's more or less verbatim from Varchi's chronicle.

Selected Bibliography

Charles Affron, *A Stage for Poets: Studies in the Theater of Hugo and Musset*, Princeton, N. J., 1971.

Didier Alexandre, "Florence *extra muros*: remarques sur l'espace dans *Lorenzaccio*," *Littératures*, 23 (1990): 117-134.

Ivan Barko and Bruce Burgess, *La Dynamique des points de vue dans le texte de théâtre: analyses de points de vue: "Le Misanthrope," "Le Mariage de Figaro," "Lorenzaccio," "En attendant Godot"*, Paris, 1988.

Jeanne Bem et al., *Musset: "Lorenzaccio," "On ne badine pas avec l'amour,"* avec la participation de la *Société des études romantiques*, Paris, c. 1990.

Paul Bénichou, *L'Ecole du désenchantement : Sainte-Beuve, Nodier, Musset, Nerval, Gautier*, Paris, c. 1992.

Ceri Crossley, *Musset, "Lorenzaccio"*, London, 1983.

Robert T. Denommé, "Chatterton, Ruy Blas, Lorenzaccio: Three Tragic Heroes," *Laurels*, 61 (1) (1990): 55-67.

Jean-Jacques Didier, *L'Esprit: stylistique du mot d'esprit dans le théâtre de Musset*, Amsterdam, 1992.

Elio de Domenico, *Musset et l'Italie;* en appendice *"L'apologie de Lorenzino de Médicis,"* Turin, 1976.

Paul Dimoff, *La Genèse de Lorenzaccio*, 2e éd. revue et corrigée, Paris, 1964.

Angelika Fabig, *Kunst und Künstler im Werk Alfred de Mussets*, Heidelberg, 1976.

Antoine-Michel Filhol, *Galerie du Musée Napoléon*, 11 volumes, Paris, 1804-1815.

Donald R. Gamble, "The Image of Italy and the Creative Imagination of Alfred de Musset," in *Proceedings of the XIIth Congress of the International Comparative Literature Association, II, Space and Boundaries in Literature*, Roger Bauer, ed., Munich, 1990.

Eric L. Gans, *Musset et le "drame tragique"; essai d'analyse paradoxale*, Paris, 1974.

Pierre Gastinel, *Le Romantisme d'Alfred de Musset*, Rouen, 1933.

Herbert Gochberg, *Stage of Dreams*, Geneva, 1967.

Charlotte F. Haldane, *Alfred; The Passionate Life of Alfred de Musset*, New York, 1960.

Alain Heyvaert, *La Transparence et l'indicible dans l'œuvre de Musset*, Paris, 1994.

Robert Horville, *"Lorenzaccio," Musset, analyse critique*, Paris, 1972.

W. D. Howarth, "Drama," in *The French Romantics*, D. G. Charlton, ed., Cambridge, 1984, pp. 205-247.

Kenneth Kraus, "Lorenzaccio, Castraccio, Lorenzetta: A Consideration of Who May Play Musset's Lorenzo," *George Sand Studies*, 10(1-2) (1990-1991): 18-27.

Léon Lafoscade, *Le Théâtre d'Alfred de Musset*, Paris, 1901 (reprinted Paris, 1966).

Henri Lefebvre, *Alfred de Musset dramaturge*, Paris, 1955.

John W. MacInnes, "*Lorenzaccio* and the Drama of Narration," in *Text and Presentation*, edited by Karelisa V. Hartigan, Lanham, MD, 1988, pp. 137-145.

Thérèse Malachy, "*Lorenzaccio*: du meurtre politique au sacrifice rituel," *Revue d'Histoire du Théâtre*, 40(3[159]) (1988): 273-280.

Cecil Malthus, Rex A. Barrell (ed.), *Musset et Shakespeare: Etude analytique de l'influence de Shakespeare sur le théâtre d'Alfred de Musset*, New York, 1988.

Bernard Masson, *Lectures de l'imaginaire*, Paris, 1993.

_____________, *Musset et le théâtre intérieur*, Paris, 1974.

_____________, *Musset et son double, lecture de Lorenzaccio*, Paris, 1978.

Joachim-Claude Merlant, *Le Moment de "Lorenzaccio" dans le destin de Musset*, Athens, 1955.

Alfred de Musset, *Œuvres complètes de A. de Musset. Comédies et Proverbes*, 2 vols., Paris, 1952.

____________, *Œuvres complètes*, texte établi et présenté par Philippe van Tieghem, Paris, 1963.

____________, *Comedies and Proverbs*, translated and with an introduction by David Sices, Baltimore, 1994.

____________, *Les Deux "André del Sarto" d'Alfred de Musset*, presented by Pierre Gastinel, Rouen, 1933.

____________, *Un Spectacle dans un fauteuil*, 2nd issue, 2 vols. (Paris, 1834): (contains: *Lorenzaccio, Les Caprices de Marianne, André del Sarto, Fantasio, On ne badine pas avec l'amour, La Nuit vénitienne*).

Paul de Musset, *Alfred de Musset, sa vie, son œuvre*, Paris, 1877.

Antonio Natali and Alessandro Cecchi, *Andrea del Sarto. Catalogo completo dei dipinti*, Florence, 1989.

Margaret A. Rees, *Alfred de Musset*, London, 1971.

Pierre-André Rieben, *Délires romantiques : Musset, Nodier, Gautier, Hugo*, Paris, 1989.

Evelyn Schels, *Die Tradition des lyrischen Dramas von Musset bis Hofsmannsthal*, Frankfurt am Main, New York, 1990.

Naomi Schor, "La pérodie: Superposition dans *Lorenzaccio*," in *Discours et pouvoir*, edited by Ross Chambers, Ann Arbor, MI, 1982, pp. 73-86.

John Shearman, *Andrea del Sarto*, 2 vol., Oxford, 1965.

Maurice Z. Shroder, *Icarus: The Image of the Artist in French Romanticism*, Cambridge, Mass., 1961.

David Sices, *Theater of Solitude. The Drama of Alfred de Musset*, Hanover, N.H., 1974.

Patricia J. Siegel, *Alfred de Musset: A Reference Guide*, Boston, 1982.

Alex Szogyi, "Musset's *Lorenzaccio*: George Sand's Ultimate Gift," in *Woman as Mediatrix: Essays on Nineteenth-Century Women Writers*, edited by Avriel H. Goldberger, Westport, CT, 1987, pp. 89-98.

Jean-Jacques Thomas, "Les maîtres-mots de Musset: Peuple et pouvoir dans *Lorenzaccio,*" in *Peuple et pouvoir: Etudes de lexicologie politique*, edited by Michel Glatigny and Jacques Guilhaumou, Lille, 1981, pp. 179-196.

Jean-Marie Thomasseau, *Alfred de Musset: "Lorenzaccio"*, Paris, 1986.

Marie Josephine Whitaker, *Lorenzo ou Lorenzaccio?: misères et splendeurs d'un héros romantique*, Paris, 1989.

Matthew H. Wikander, "The Revolution of the Times: Musset, Büchner, and Brecht," in Wikander, *The Play of Truth and State: Historical Drama from Shakespeare to Brecht*, Baltimore, 1986, pp. 197-240.

Currents in Comparative Romance Languages and Literatures

This series was founded in 1987, and actively solicits book-length manuscripts (approximately 200–400 pages) which treat aspects of Romance Languages and Literatures. Originally established for works dealing with two or more Romance literatures, the series has broadened its horizons and now includes studies on themes within a single literature or between different literatures, civilizations, art, music, film and social movements, as well as comparative linguistics. Studies on individual writers with an influence on other literatures/civilizations are also welcome. We entertain a variety of approaches and formats, provided the scholarship and methodology are appropriate.

For additional information about the series or for the submission of manuscripts, please contact:

Tamara Alvarez-Detrell and Michael G. Paulson
c/o Dr. Heidi Burns
Peter Lang Publishing, Inc.
516 N. Charles St.
2nd Floor
Baltimore, MD 21201